Arnold Palmer

Homespun Stories of The King

CHRIS RODELL

TRIUMPH
B O O K S

Names: Rodell, Chris, author.
Title: Arnold Palmer : homespun stories of the king / Chris Rodell.
Description: Chicago, Illinois : Triumph Books, 2018.
Identifiers: LCCN 2017046520 | ISBN 9781629375687 (paperback)
Subjects: LCSH: Palmer, Arnold, 1929-2016. | Golfers—United States—
    Biography. | BISAC: SPORTS & RECREATION / Golf. | TRAVEL /
    United States / Northeast / Middle Atlantic (NJ, NY, PA).
Classification: LCC GV964.P3 R64 2018 | DDC 796.352092 [B]—dc23
LC record available at https://lccn.loc.gov/2017046520Printed in U.S.A.

This book is available in quantity at special discounts for your group or organization. For further information, contact:

Triumph Books LLC
814 North Franklin Street
Chicago, Illinois 60610
(312) 337-0747
www.triumphbooks.com

Printed in U.S.A.
ISBN: 978-1-62937-568-7
Design by Florence Aliesch

For past reveries, current considerations, and future frolics, this book is dedicated to the inimitable Michael Patrick Shiels.

Contents

Foreword

Would Arnold Palmer have become Arnold Palmer without his hometown of Latrobe, Pennsylvania? Or to paraphrase what Winnie Palmer once said of her husband, "I can't decide if he's simply complex or complexly simple." Could it be both?

For this book Chris Rodell, a popular author and Latrobe resident since 1992, interviewed more than 200 area neighbors and began each interview with a simple request: "Please tell me your best Arnold Palmer story." You're holding the responses right in your hand. This book takes the exuberant nitty-gritty of what they had to say about the man they knew and shines a light on their experiences to reveal something beautiful to behold. Because the story of Arnold Palmer and his beloved Latrobe isn't just some story of hometown roots. No, dig a little deeper, and it's a story of community, encouragement, optimism, determination, and cheerful perseverance in the face of all life's challenges.

So, at its heart, the story of Palmer and Latrobe is a story about the United States of America. It details the benefits of what happens when individuals and their communities mutually decide to be good for goodness' sake. Because the Latrobe that raised and supported Palmer likely differs little from the place you call home. It has solid industry, good schools, strong communities of various faiths, recreational opportunities and is populated by many good-hearted people who work hard and play hard. That probably sounds familiar. Every state in America has dozens of small towns that fit that description, and many are still producing people of character, faith, and genuine appreciation for their country.

But there might just be something special about Latrobe. After all, Palmer isn't the only beloved star who called it home. Mister Fred Rogers was born in Latrobe. So were Rolling Rock beer and professional football. For more than 50 years, Latrobe and St. Vincent College have been the summer home to the six-time Super Bowl champion Pittsburgh Steelers. And every August Latrobe celebrates its role in being the birthplace of one of the most famous desserts, when it hosts the Great American Banana Split Festival.

Palmer was first and foremost a professional golfer, but more importantly he was generous, thoughtful, funny, inspirational, and a friend to many. He was equally at ease dining with kings and queens as he was having shots and beers with the gang sitting around the bar at the local volunteer fire department social hall.

He could be difficult and demanding, but to me he simply was a dear friend for more than 60 years. We laughed together but also cried together. Like anybody, we had our differences, but these never stood in the way of our relationship. And he was blessed with charm, charisma, and patience. Such an inspirational man, he certainly lived his life to the fullest. No matter what the circumstance, his effort was relentless—even when the odds were stacked against him. He was a world traveler who gave every appearance he'd have been content being a Latrobe homebody. He was a record-setting aviator with a large personality who somehow managed to remain grounded. And maybe Latrobe and its people were the reason he remained so grounded. He never forgot who he was and where he came from.

Maybe it was destiny that Rodell, a writer who's become known for observational humor, moved to Latrobe 26 years ago with zero professional interest in pestering his famous neighbor. Coincidental circumstance led him to a neighborly friendship and to Palmer eventually providing his official cover endorsement on Rodell's previous book. The book's topic? How to be happier.

So, of course, Palmer was supportive. Making the world a happier place was what he'd been doing his entire life. He did it with hospitals and philanthropic organizations in Orlando, Florida, and he did it with people who lived just down the street. Heck, he did it every time he signed his name in that indelibly flawless penmanship. He was doing it right up to the day he died.

I'm confident fans will enjoy this euphoric book that doesn't stop at celebrating the life of another famous man. It provides evidence that some greatness comes naturally while some is forged. My hope is that this magic will continue all across the United States for many years to come. And as this book makes clear, it can happen in hearts all around the world.

—Gary Player

Introduction

The second most common question asked of people who live in Latrobe, Pennsylvania, as my wife and I have done since 1992, is, "Have you met Arnold Palmer?" Through the 26 years, my answer has changed by dramatic degrees. For nearly 10 years, my answer was a grinding no, a truthfulness that always left the questioner disappointed and me feeling diminished. It was a social failure. Living in Latrobe and not knowing Arnold Palmer was like living at the North Pole and not knowing Santa Claus.

We finally and formally met—introductory handshake, eye contact, and a concluding thumbs-up—in 2001. A hometown box had been checked after nine years. But it was a meeting without zest, zip, or zing. It was as if we'd shared a cab ride to a bus station, not a hometown. It left me in a weakened position to answer what is the No. 1 most common question, which is, "So what's Arnold Palmer really like?"

I'd say I've been told he's cool, fun, and friendly, but in truth I hadn't the foggiest idea. My answer for years would have been dismissed by any fair court as hearsay. Then on August 2, 2005, circumstances beyond my control changed my life, both professionally and personally in ways both silly and profound. I began getting paid to immerse myself in the daily details of Palmer's entire life. I was hired to go through more than a dozen legal-sized cardboard boxes stuffed with newspaper and magazine clippings, etc., detailing every time Palmer's name made the news anywhere in the world. Each box had thousands of clips, some momentous, others minuscule. For transcription purposes, I'd pore over nearly 40 years of date books. I'd read boxes of fan letters and whole newspapers and magazines devoted to Latrobe's favorite son. Know what I'd do if I had a question? I'd ask Mr. Palmer.

And the formal honorific is deliberate. Calling him Arnie, Arnold, or—heaven forbid—Arn would seem as inappropriate to me as calling The King "Sweetheart," even though that description would have been perfectly accurate.

Overall, I'd spend more than 100 hours over the next 11 years, not as his buddy, but as the guy privileged with the liberty to ask him anything that popped into my head. Sure, we talked about golf, aviation, history, architecture, nature, politics, loss, failure, and what happens when we die, but the undercurrent of each of those questions was much bigger than all that.

We talked about life.

It gave me foundational insights I could use any time some curious stranger asked me that No. 1 question: what's Arnold Palmer really like? "Arnold Palmer is perfectly cool, authentic, and refreshing. If Arnold Palmer were a drink, he'd be an Arnold Palmer," I'd say.

If Arnold Palmer were the only member of The Greatest Generation, it would still be The Greatest Generation solely because it included Arnold Palmer. He's often referred to as a legendary golfer. The description doesn't begin to do justice to the momentous legacy.

I smugly believed mine was the best answer. In fact, I don't think I really knew at all what Arnold Palmer was really like until I asked all his Latrobe neighbors to tell me what they thought Arnold Palmer was really like. You're holding the sum answer in your hands.

I hope my role in this doesn't confuse anyone into thinking I'm claiming I was a Palmer insider, confidant, or buddy. I was graciously allowed to bask within the Palmer solar system, but, really, to extend that astronomical analogy, I was Pluto, and experts today argue whether Pluto's even a planet. But I'm friends with many of the people who truly were his devoted friends. Some of their best stories follow this introduction.

At heart, I consider myself a guy who was blessed to spend many delightful hours chatting with a delightful and historic individual—indeed, a friend—who just happened to be Arnold Palmer. That I feel very lucky about my situation, I hope, comes shining through loud and clear on the following pages.

Sure, I wish I'd known him better. I wish he'd have called me for days of golf, drinks, and dinner. I wish he'd have rung me up and said, "Hey, Chris, ol' buddy! I'm flying to Augusta for a quick 18. Wanna tag along?" I wish I could write a book that honestly states Arnold Palmer and I were the very best of friends.

And, man, I wish he was still around.

Chapter 1

Mr. Palmer's Neighborhood

It was 1994 when the saucy old, widowed lady next door surprised me when she said she spent a lot of time watching televised golf. Then she about shocked all the hairs off my head when she confided the reason why.

She used to spend hours and hours with her hands deep in Arnold Palmer's pants. "He always paid me," she said matter-of-factly. "To me, he was just another customer. His office called a while back, but I told them I don't do that kind of thing anymore."

She was Palmer's seamstress, something I'd never known in the two years she and I had lived next door to one another on Arnold Palmer Drive, one-half mile from Latrobe Country Club and the humble home of Palmer himself. Her casual mention inspired a giddy impulse to dash inside and phone five friends who mistook my breathlessness to mean I'd sired triplets to supermodels. It was a sound indicator why I was sure I'd never fit in as a year-round resident of the birthplace of the venerable gent. In the birthplace and residence of one of America's biggest deals, the man himself was no big deal.

And that's just the way he liked it.

The lesson became clear when many years later and after nearly 100 hours of one-on-one time with the man himself, I learned what little value he placed on puffy flattery. I started one of our in-depth interviews by saying how much I enjoyed hearing his historic insights during our breezy little sessions. He responded: "And I can't tell you how much I enjoy you coming in here to blow so much sweet smoke up my ass!"

He made that off-color remark in 2007 just two days after dining with Queen Elizabeth at the White House of George W. Bush. I kept waiting for the day he'd ask me to pull his finger.

That Palmer felt that comfortable talking that way to me would have floored my late father. Paul Rodell's contribution to history's most pivotal conflict was to serve our country as a U.S. Navy chaplain's assistant. It's almost impossible to conjure a less perilous title for a World War II veteran. Maybe Army pillow tester? That's why his stories as a foot soldier in Arnie's Army struck his sons as more stirring than his days dusting bibles on behalf of God and Uncle Sam.

He got sunburned at Oakmont in '62. Stiff new golf shoes blistered his feet on a long march following Palmer at Firestone in '75. He caught hell for spilling beer on the couch reaching for Kleenex to mop away tears when Palmer crossed the Swilcan Burn for the last time in '95. I was raised with a reverence for the man I still, out of respect, refer to as Mr. Palmer.

But that's not why I moved to tiny Youngstown, Pennsylvania (me and the 326 other locals are always snobbishly informing strangers that Mr. Palmer's Latrobe Country Club is actually in Youngstown, 15696, not Latrobe, 15650).

I was a general assignment newspaper reporter in a small Latrobe bureau office that was right next door to B.C. Kenly's, a friendly tavern that served 50-cent Rolling Rock drafts. The buildings were a well-struck 3 wood from Latrobe Brewing Company. I was assigned to cover local school boards, city council, and the daily doings of small town life. When my wife-to-be and I were searching for an area home, it seemed prudent to move to a place that

From left to right, Peg, Winnie, Arnold, and Amy Palmer pose during the 1970s. *(Howdy Giles)*

in those days of Y2K computer bug hysteria assured convenient access to a brewery that produced good, cheap beer.

But the real reason we moved here was the same one Palmer cited as the reason he never left: we're both fond of the folks. They are tough, no-nonsense people who work hard and play hard. "Latrobe, that old steel town, is the crucible that forged Arnold Palmer," says Jim Nantz, the Palmer confidant and CBS Sports announcer who'd go an hour out of his way to visit Palmer anytime marquee competition took him to Pittsburgh.

I knew what he meant. Latrobe is populated by the kind of men and women you need to mold an enduring American icon. They're the quirky, no-nonsense people he never left behind. The story of Latrobe and Arnold Palmer is the story of how one small town and a big time celebrity forever bonded to forge a mutually beneficial relationship admired around the world. Palmer gushed about Latrobe, it seems, specifically because the folks here never really gushed about him. Neither Latrobe nor Palmer took the other for granted, but neither took one another too seriously either. It was a mutual love that was engrained but never enforced.

A man known for hitching his pants never, in the watchful eyes of observant locals, ever got too big for his britches. Why would this legendary man, feted in glitzy palaces around the world, choose to live in a humble Western Pennsylvania shot-and-a-beer town just 320 yards from the drafty little shack where he was born?

It was a question I'd yet to ask when my then-girlfriend (and eventual bride) Valerie and I moved into 505 Main Street and I began a career of writing general feature stories for various national magazines. It wasn't until the local council changed my address to Arnold Palmer Drive that I began to concentrate on golf writing. Palmer is not tiny Youngstown's only claim to fame. The rest of Main Street was renamed in honor of another famous resident, the late Mister Fred Rogers, a schoolmate of Palmer's. At the time I could leave my front door and turn left and be on Arnold Palmer Drive or turn right and stroll down Fred Rogers Way.

Alas, my golf game still tends to trend after Mister Rogers. It is gentle, unfailingly polite, and is something grown up meanies make vicious fun of. But none of that stopped me from seizing the Palmer connection. "I may never be the best golf writer," I reasoned, "but I can be the only one on Arnold Palmer Drive just down the street from Latrobe Country Club and Arnold Palmer himself."

Even before employing that little professional conceit, I was awestruck every single time I had a brush with Palmer, a small town neighbor who didn't know me from the biblical Adam. I'd slow the car to a crawl when I'd see him teeing up on the club's roadside 117-yard par-3 second hole—he'd aced it four times—in the hopes I'd see some magic. A courteous motorist, he once waved me through a stale yellow light. I must have run five senior citizens and a school bus full of frightened toddlers off the road on my mad rush to the bar to spill the news to my buddies.

And I was among the small gallery at Laurel Valley Golf Club for the Pennsylvania Classic two weeks after September 11, 2001, and saw Palmer make deliberate and bracing eye contact with every one of us while his forgettable partners teed off. In those still-fragile days, his lingering eyes seemed to convey encouraging strength. I understood that day the messianic charisma that's inspired a nation for more than 50 years.

I remember the sunny Saturday morning outside the Youngstown Post Office, a small town social center, when my wife and I were approached by a striking autumn-haired woman with a soft spot for golden retrievers like the one tugging at the end of our leash. "He is magnificent," she gushed, luxuriously kneading both hands deep into Casey's fur. "Oh, you must have him come and meet our Prince! Please call. It will be so much fun!"

We promised we would. After she'd skipped away, my wife asked the identity of the bubbly stranger. "That's Mrs. Winnie Walzer Palmer," I said. "She married young Arnold on December 20, 1954, the same day as my own father and mother were married. When my old man heard the coincidental news and sent them an anniversary card, Winnie responded the next five years with ones of her own."

I called a week later but was told she wasn't feeling well. It was 1998. We didn't know it, but she was suffering from the cancer that would defeat her in November 1999.

I remember being steadfastly mystified by local reporters, chums all, who treated their frequent dealings with Palmer the way I used to treat the hapless punching bags who were appointed to the local municipal authority board. I understood a certain professional detachment was necessary to cover a subject, but this wasn't some politician seeking our dollars and votes. This wasn't some preening movie star posing as an action hero out to charm the ticket-buying public.

This was Arnold Palmer.

Thus, I was terrified that someday I'd be called upon in a professional capacity to interview Mr. Palmer because I believed my most pointed question would be along the lines of: "What's it like to be so great? And, please, try to be honest…unless you don't feel like it." I was convinced my story would read, "It's been five hours since I was privileged to sit down and meet the great Arnold Palmer. My right hand is still tingling from his introductory greeting. My fair and balanced conclusion is as such: this man is far too accomplished to have to submit to silly questions from impudent reporters like myself."

I understood such gushing would earn widespread ridicule from industry colleagues. I'd be finished, unemployable, a lonely ghost rattling through the cobwebbed house with no prospects and nothing but time to dream in vain of better days that would never dawn.

It didn't matter. I figured I'd never be in a position to interview Palmer. Editors whom I worked for understood I was more comfortable in the company of caddies than kings. And even if I did and was unable to further function as a professional journalist, I knew the failing would leave me plenty of time to learn how to work a sewing machine.

I knew the neighborhood was in need of another seamstress. Little did I know then how circumstance would lead me to within reach of

Palmer's inner circle, how he'd confide in me, how he'd volunteer to write the foreword and cover endorsement for my silly *Crayons!* book, and how his top business officer told me three days after Palmer's death that my intimate stories about Palmer had made me the de facto spokesman for Arnie's Army. He was weeping as he said this. The emotional revelation left me feeling startled. Could it be true?

I was thinking of all this, this surreal journey, on October 4, 2016, as I watched Palmer pilot Pete Luster fly Palmer's Citation X through the cloud-flecked skies above Latrobe for one last time. My wife and I had been invited to attend the celebrity-studded memorial at St. Vincent College. I had a story to tell, a story about a big-time guy who never once thought of leaving the small town that shaped him. It is a euphoric story, one told with much love, joy, and appreciation for both the man and the town. The tricky part, as always, would be telling such a story without blowing too much sweet smoke up anybody's ass.

It is a kingdom so minuscule, so inconspicuous, many of those who traverse it on a daily basis fail to grasp its significance or existence even. It's an uneven two-lane road that leads from a country road to a one-stoplight town that lacks the regal structures, parade ground stables, gilded trappings of royalty or any dwelling refined observers would consider palatial.

There's a post office, an entrance to the local high school, a volunteer firehouse, a monument to local veterans, a snappy diner, an art gallery, some ball fields, a disproportionate number of friendly taverns, a few restaurants, and rows of two-story homes that can be described with adjectives ranging from immaculate to dilapidated and most everything in between. It's just a good, old, small American town, one where nearly every utility pole is proudly festooned year-round with the flag. In many ways it may be indistinguishable from the town you call home.

But on that otherwise nondescript little street once lived a man considered around the world to be The King, and it was here on this 1.6-mile stretch he could look and see everything he ever needed. There was history, recreation, productivity, commerce, conviviality, and, oh, man, there were friends.

Understand, this is not Latrobe. It is—to further muddle everything you've ever heard about Arnold Palmer—Youngstown. The name is redundant enough that all the signs for the hometown Youngstown Grille emphasize you're in Youngstown, Pennsylvania, ("not Ohio").

It's one of those geographic anomalies that to get to the Latrobe Country Club you have to depart actual Latrobe and drive 3.5 miles south across U.S. Route 30 to Youngstown, and, of course, you can't get to Latrobe Country Club without traversing at least some of Arnold Palmer Drive, and that's the only thing about the conundrum that makes perfect sense.

Even without Palmer, you could contend the town is deceptively special. It is home to not one but two thriving technology leaders—Kennametal and Westmoreland Mechanical Testing and Research—whose innovative fingerprints are on equipment all around the world and far, far above it. Both have contributed breakthroughs that wound up enhancing safety features on the International Space Station. Aggressive Grinding Service has been a North American leader in precision carbide grinding and ceramic finishing since 1988. That's a lot of international productivity for a town of just 326 to export. Of course, even those titans can't claim to be Youngstown's greatest export.

That flesh-and-blood export grew up in a drafty old house along 9 Mile Run creek near what today is the tee to Latrobe Country Club's 5th hole. So if the wind was just right, and his aim was true, this man, who'd been around the world too many times to count, could have hit the back porch of the home in which he was born with a drive struck from the front porch of the home where he was living the week he passed away 87 years later.

He told me in '10 of his childhood memories of that first home: "It was really an old farm house from before they built the golf course. It was rickety but wonderful. I remember the snows would come in through the windows. I'd wake up in the morning, and there was snow on the bed. I'd pump well water from the kitchen to the basement for my mother to do laundry. Then it was hung out to dry right there beside the old 6th hole. That's the way it was. We had pigs and chickens in the backyard and every fall we'd butcher the pigs for food. That was in the '30s, during the Depression."

Palmer bought the club and all its property in 1971. He spent three years weighing what to do with the old home before deciding it had to go. "I gave serious thought to fixing it up, but it would have been so expensive that it wasn't worth it. Pennsylvania governor Raymond Shafer wanted to keep it and preserve it as a historic site. Now, I wish I had done just that. If I had to do over, I would have kept it."

His answer had me bust out laughing. "C'mon!" I said. "Who do you think you're kidding? You'd right away move back in and resume living there, bed snows and all!" He laughed sheepishly, nearly blushed, like I'd caught Palmer in a lie. It's a fact that since he became a wage-earning adult in 1955, Palmer's had just three primary residences in his entire life, and they've all been within 320 yards of the house in which he was born. Heck, given that kind of hometown devotion, local leaders would have been justified in renaming the main street Arnold Palmer Drive for no other reason than Palmer's civic steadfastness.

And the ceremonial street signs aren't the only place on the short drive you'll find his name. The western end of Arnold Palmer Drive forms a T at the end of the auxiliary runway for the Arnold Palmer Regional Airport, which was named in 1999. The entrance is farther south and leads visitors and tourists to a namesake statue of Palmer leaning on a golf club. Built of bronze and dedicated in 2007, it's a rare example of something immovable still capable of swaggering.

Many tourists and executives landing at Arnold Palmer naturally check into the SpringHill Suites by Marriott right on the airport end of Arnold Palmer Drive. Co-owned by Palmer and Marriott, the hotel's decor is a lavish tribute to Palmer. Before they both died 55 days apart in the fall of 2016, Arnold and his brother Jerry, who was 15 years younger, were often found having drinks and entertaining guests in the lobby bar.

Jerry had been the general manager at his brother's club. At one time a turkey farm, his home was on the street named for his brother, and there were many days when his sole method of transportation was a club golf cart he'd use to get from home to the club—the 16th tee was his back yard—and back again.

Jerry and I were friends who enjoyed golfing and drinking together. If that makes it sound like I'm being boastfully exclusive with that statement, allow me to clarify. Jerry enjoyed golfing and drinking with everyone he met. The Palmers were convivial people in a convivial town. If anyone made eye contact with either of them, they were likely to get a warm handshake, some pleasant conversation, and maybe a new friend.

It was like that at places like Falbo's Rainbow Inn or The Tin Lizzy. Youngstown, you see, is one of those rambunctious western Pennsylvania towns that may have just one stop light, but it is blessed with seven places to get something to drink. And not one of them, including Latrobe

Country Club, looks glitzy enough to lure millionaires—much less a man who was at the time of his death estimated to be worth 700 times that. *Forbes* magazine estimates Palmer earned $42 million—42 years after his last professional victory earned him a first place check of $32,000—in 2015.

Yet, each of these Youngstown taverns, as well as many others in Latrobe and the surrounding communities, has stories about the times Arnold Palmer stopped by for drinks or a bite to eat. "Oh, both he and Jerry used to come here all the time," said Buck Pawlosky, Tin Lizzy owner since 1980. "Arnold would meet everyone who wanted to say hello. He'd take pictures with everyone who wanted. I remember the time he bought cakes and handed them out to all the children. The whole place would light up when he'd walk in. He was the greatest. He was beloved around the world, but he had this way of making everyone he met feel like they were the special ones."

What is it about this place that exerted such an intangible pull on a man who'd never lack for regal alternatives? I asked him that in a '10 interview. He said: "This is the most beautiful place in the world. It has everything. It has mountains, fresh water, four beautiful seasons, and friendly people. I've been all over the world and have never found a place better than this. I live in Florida the rest of the time and I love Orlando, but if I were forced to choose one place over all the others, this would be it. I never once thought of leaving. And I never will."

It was a commitment he kept until September 25, 2016. And it is notable how in the last seven or so years of his life how the famous globetrotter became more and more of a homebody, increasingly content with simple fare, familiar surroundings, and friendly acquaintances he'd known for decades. And when he no longer felt compelled to go to the world, the world came to him.

Chapter 2

Meeting the Man

The first time I remember interviewing Arnold Palmer, it had very little to do with him being Arnold Palmer. In fact, it had to do with romance. But it being Arnold Palmer, the romance involved a little golf. It was at Laurel Valley Golf Club in Ligonier, about 12 miles east of Latrobe, Pennsylvania. Built in 1959 to be a sort of Augusta National North, Palmer was one of nine men who oversaw its creation. In fact, most every PGA Tour program at tournaments where Palmer played over the years say, "Arnold Palmer, Laurel Valley G.C.," not Latrobe C.C. The luscious course hosted the 1965 PGA Championship, the 1975 Ryder Cup, the 1989 Senior U.S. Open and the 2005 Senior PGA Championship. I was there for the 2001 Pennsylvania Classic to do oddball features for *Golf* magazine.

In 2000 *Golf* magazine made me a staff writer. They greenlit my story idea about asking professional golfers to recall their first aces, so I had a bona fide reason to spend the week at Laurel that fall of 2001. The tournament had been delayed a week because of the 9/11 attacks. The tournament wasn't a marquee event, so many of the big names weren't there. I talked to Bo Van Pelt, Kelly Gibson, Bob Estes, Stan

Author Chris Rodell stands in between two Latrobe, Pennsylvania, luminaries—Arnold Palmer and Palmer's personal assistant, Doc Giffin— that he befriended. (Chris Rodell)

Utley, and a few others. All told interesting stories. A hole in one, even to professional golfers, is very special, or as Mac Grady said: "A hole in one is amazing when you think of all the different universes through which this white mass of molecules must pass on its way to the bottom of the cup."

But I wasn't thinking physics when I saw Palmer uncharacteristically alone on his way to the practice range carrying his own bag. I remember being pleased to add a legend's name to my otherwise indistinguishable roster of journeymen. I asked if he had time for a question. "Shoot," he said.

And there was just something about him. He'd been asked so many questions about so many topics that I felt a straightforward approach was unworthy. I decided to try to tease some fun out of him. So instead of asking him to tell me about his first ace, I put an artful spin on it: "Which do you remember more clearly: your first ace or your first kiss?"

He stopped but didn't hesitate. "Oh," he said, "the first ace."

How come? "It just meant so much more to me," he said, laughing. It was a hearty laugh, too. Clearly not a mere chuckle. More of a bubbly guffaw.

I'd made Arnold Palmer laugh! I couldn't wait to tell my old man. I had no way of knowing it, but in five years, I'd become the expert on Palmer's 20 aces. We talked for about five minutes. He told me about a few years before when he, Jack Nicklaus, and Gary Player had been strolling down a fairway during The Tradition, and the topic came up. Palmer said at the time he'd had 17. Nicklaus said he, too, had 17. You're not going to believe it, Player said, but I've had 17, too. The legendary threesome marveled at the odd coincidence.

Doc Giffin is to me a legend in his own right. In 1966 Palmer asked the former sportswriter for the *Pittsburgh Press* to be his personal assistant. At the time Doc had been enjoying a fun and stable career as the press secretary for the PGA Tour. People asked why Giffin would want to leave the prestigious position to work for a golfer whose career would soon conclude. What would he do when Palmer's popularity began to diminish?

But Doc obviously made a wise call. In addition to that great judgment call he made, Doc was renown, Doc was proper, and Doc could be a little scary. He was Arnold Palmer's consigliere. Everyone who wanted something from Palmer—and that was a significant part of the population—had to go through Doc. From a distance, he had reason to view me leerily, too. "I thought it was terrible news when I heard a writer for *Golf* magazine was living right up the street," he later confided. "I thought you'd be here all the time nosing around for Arnold Palmer tips and stories."

He had me figured all wrong. In fact, for the next few years, the only time I'd stop in the office was for yearly Christmas courtesy calls to deliver two *Amazing But True Golf Facts* page-a-day calendars—one for Doc, one for the Boss. My author/friend Allan Zullo asked me to help produce them. That meant culling through hundreds of golf-related websites, magazines, and sports sections each year to relate more than 300 interesting or amusing facts and quotes for publication. Here's an example, one of just 5,250 I'd composed from 1999 to 2015: "Charles Anthony came to the final hole of the 2012 Rhode Island Junior PGA Championship trailing leader Steve Letterle by 2 strokes. A difficult task, but certainly not unprecedented. What made it even tougher was the final hole at Montaup CC in Portsmouth was a par-4, 304-yarder, one that would be difficult for Letterle to do worse than bogie. What did Anthony do? Just aced the hole! Talk about putting pressure on your opponent."

Doc would tell me how much Palmer appreciated the book and these facts. I thought he was just being polite. It wasn't until 2006 when I'd begun interviewing Palmer with some regularity that I saw with my own eyes he was serious. There was my page-a-day calendar square in the middle of Palmer's desk right where lesser mortals keep things like desktop computers. Palmer was reading my convenience store Confusionisms first thing every day. It struck me that it would be like Elvis waking up and playing a commercial jingle I'd written just because he thought the tune was catchy.

I used to sit and wonder who'd revel in so much arcane golf trivia. I'd wonder about the characteristics of what kind of golf nut so relied on daily golf trivia to propel the calendar into one of the best selling in industry history. I was floored when I realized that primary golf nut was Palmer. He just ate it all up. "Not only am I a reader," he said reaching into his desk and fanning out a thick stack of past pages, "but I keep a bunch of them for reference purposes. I'm always telling people about something I've found in these. They're great!"

In fact, Palmer became the primary reason I continued doing the calendars about five years after I first thought about quitting them. I didn't want to disappoint my most loyal reader. But I began to dread the task as the humble golf calendars began turning me into a monster and an impossibly annoying golf partner. Any casual comment would launch a tidal wave of meaningless golf trivia. I know the first metal golf wood was used in 1891, that the world's longest golf course was 8,335 yards long and was in tiny Massachusetts, and that Gary Player only eats bacon when he thinks no one is watching.

A friend said his bladder was full and he couldn't hold it till we got to the clubhouse. I responded: "Did you know that when it comes to holding it, nobody can beat Jim Thorpe, and I'm talking about holding golf balls. His hands are so big he can hold eight golf balls upside down with each mitt. Thorpe is the ninth of 12 children born in Roxboro, North Carolina. His dad was a local green superintendent. He spent one year in prison for tax evasion but is still beloved for his community generosity."

The guy said I talked too much. I asked if he was insinuating I was in violation of obscure USGA Golf Rule 33.7, which relates to golfers who intentionally disturb or distract opponents by excessive talking.

He told me to go jump in a lake. I said that might be a lucrative proposition. "Did you know that golf ball lake recovery divers can earn as much as $100,000 a year? That's a lot of money, sure, but it's very treacherous work. I can tell you story after story of lake divers who've been attacked by alligators, snakes, and rabid beavers."

I never knew when to shut off. And putting the calendar together was all-consuming. The new template would arrive each June, and I'd stare with angst at all the blank pages. I'd usually spread it out over three or four months, but the thought of it was always with me. My record was 2008 when I did the whole calendar in three weeks.

post
office
box
fifty-two
youngstown,
pennsylvania
15696

December 23, 2008

Dear Chris:

Many thanks for the calendar. You do know how much I enjoy reading the amazing golf facts each day. Even when the day is done, I tear off the page and keep it for future reference.

My very best wishes to you and your family for a Happy Holiday.

Sincerely,

Arnold

AP:gwv

Mr. Chris Rodell
2120 Lincoln Avenue
Latrobe, PA 15650

Anyhow, Doc began to realize I wasn't a threat to his orderly world. I wasn't an aggressive snoop, a pushy jerk, or the kind of writer who was eager to advance his career on Palmer's neighborly legend. I'd drift in every couple of months or so at the behest of *Golf* magazine editors wanting one or two lines from The King to add cache to an otherwise mundane story. My first ever sit-down interview in Palmer's office was a snoozer involving Palmer's historic rivalry with Nicklaus. Yawn. Nothing I could ask him would startle his intellect or yield any fresh insights. He'd heard it all before.

The whole interview took about five minutes, and Palmer barely looked up from his primary task, which was signing autographs. It was later I'd learn he'd spend as much as three hours a day signing his name in that impeccably legible stroke. Surgeons suturing scars on supermodels are less careful than Palmer was with a pen. Ensuing interviews followed suit with me playing the role of worshipful scribe, and Palmer dutifully answering questions he'd answered a million times before while rarely looking up from his daily task of autographing. My late father's golden adorations haunted the room.

That all began to change the day I went to interview him about a mulligan. His dog, Mulligan, to be precise. *Golf* magazine was doing a spread about golfers and their dogs. They asked me to talk to Palmer. To be honest, it seemed like another snoozer. I was eager to add some spice to what could be mundane. I figured I'd challenge him right away. "So," I asked, "what's an old rules stickler like you doing with a dog named Mulligan?"

Engaged, he set down his pen, looked me square in the eye, and said, "Hey, there's nothing wrong with a mulligan during a friendly round. It's a first tee custom here at Latrobe. Everyone's allowed to start the round with a mulligan."

He lamented that Mulligan was a lousy on-course dog who chased the balls and slobbered them all up. "Probably because at least once a day, I take him out back and hit a tennis ball with my sand wedge off the tee behind my office," Palmer said. "He'd chase balls all day. Man, that dog can really fly. Guaranteed, you'll never find a single worthless cat that can do that!"

I was seized by the kind of impetuosity they warn you against in disciplined journalism schools. "Oh, yeah? I'd like to see that," I said.

His eyes took on a devilish gleam, and he said, "C'mon!"

Two questions into it, the interview was over. We became two kids who'd cut class. We jawed about politics, history, and baseball. He uttered a reflexive profanity about the lowly home team when I said I saw he'd gone to a recent Pittsburgh Pirates game. He always sat in the first row right behind home plate, which meant he was always on TV, and friends would text me observations like, "Looks like he went with the nachos this time."

It was such friendly and casual chat that I felt it necessary to remind myself I was yapping with Arnold Palmer. I steered the conversation back to golf. I told him I'd snagged an invitation to play Oakmont Country Club the next day and asked if he had any suggestions about how I could get a good score that day. "I'd suggest," he said, "you play someplace else."

He was serious. And correct. It is impossible for a golfer like me to get a good score at Oakmont. But I finally had my Palmer story. I finally had an answer to the question we in Latrobe are most asked: "What's Arnold Palmer really like?"

We'd shot the bull—and there's no better phrase for it—for about 20 minutes. Just me and him. And it was unique. How many could say they saw him playing fetch with his dog, a pitching wedge, and a slobber-sogged tennis ball?

I learned a little about Mulligan that day—but a lot about Palmer. This King had a lot of jester just below the surface. He liked to laugh and joke and didn't take himself as seriously as the rest of us did. And if someone offered a chance to liberate him from something chore-like, he'd snatch it quick as could be. He was comfortable, sure, with business talk, but this was a man who preferred friendly and sometimes ribald banter. So in many ways, Palmer was just like me and you.

I'd had my long-awaited breakthrough with Palmer, but a personal connection with his most trusted lieutenant remained elusive. Doc still seemed suspicious. I think it was because he was mostly used to dealing with pedigreed golf writers, seasoned men who were well-versed in golf history, architecture, and insider customs. They travel in packs to the world's best resorts and courses, share common gossip, and become fiercely protective anytime a fledgling newcomer threatens to encroach on their privileged beats. Maybe he was just curious or polite, but one day he called and asked if I wanted to join him at Latrobe Country Club for the monthly men's stag function. It was my first time anyone had invited me to play on the course where Palmer learned the game.

Even by demanding Western Pennsylvania standards, Latrobe CC can be exceptionally brutal. It has steep hills, treacherous greens with deceptive false fronts, and claustrophobic fairways that make bowling lanes seem roomy. It doesn't make many top 10 lists, but its allure to devoted golfers is primal. This is where Palmer learned to hit the bold shots—the low cuts, the high draws—that transformed a country club kitten of a sport and bestowed it with so much heady testosterone.

So, of course, I played pathetically. My tee shots, when they didn't dribble, featured long gentle fades that rustled the leaves but barely scared the squirrels. My short game was even lousier. On the greens I was a walking yipfest. I was an embarrassment. If I was ever going to impress Doc, it wouldn't be with anything I could or couldn't do with a golf club in my hands.

Had I known the best way for someone like me to impress someone like Doc, I would never have accepted his invitation to golf. I'd have cut out the middle man and gone straight for the booze because I didn't impress Doc until the 19th hole. We were standing at the bar and Doc—still formal, still proper, still unsmiling, said—"Chris, what'll you have?"

I looked the pretty bartender in the eye and said loud and clear, "I'll have a double Jack Daniel's on the rocks, no straw." Now, I don't know if our relationship would have still flourished had I said, "Coors Light," or "White Zinfandel." All I know is my double Jack, no straw caused Doc to light up and look me over with new eyes. He beamed, exclaiming: "My man!" At that moment this revered and distinguished gentleman and I became like-minded pals.

Not long after that, I was visiting him in his office and enjoying a warm chat—I swear, good bourbon could heal the world—and I asked if he was going to watch that evening's Pirates game. He said, "No, I will not. It's Wednesday, and on Wednesday I never miss Jeff Probst and *Survivor.*"

"My man!" I said. To this day, we usually de-brief every Thursday about the previous evening's *Survivor* episode.

★★★★

I still remember the date of August 2, 2005, because I still have the hat it's stitched on. It was conveyed to me by a *Golf* magazine editor that Palmer was hosting a conference involving all his business enterprises at Latrobe Country Club. "They've asked us to cover it," my editor said. "So can you go up there for two days, introduce yourself, and let everyone know *Golf* magazine thought this shindig was important

Latrobe, Pennsylvania, residents Winnie and Arnold Palmer were married for 45 years. (*Howdy Giles*)

enough to send a reporter? Just mingle, eat the free food, and drink the free booze, and we'll pay you $300. Can you do it?"

Like any golf writer, I responded: "Will there be free golf?"

"Of course!"

"I'll do it!"

They'd come from all over the world. The club was closed two days to accommodate squads of cheerful men and women who were there representing Arnold Palmer course designers, Arnold Palmer dog collar makers, Arnold Palmer card games, Arnold Palmer teas, Arnold Palmer restaurants, Arnold Palmer suspenders and sportswear. The ample swag bags included snazzy Arnold Palmer neckties, Arnold Palmer umbrellas, Arnold Palmer stationery, Arnold Palmer divot repair tools, Arnold Palmer magazines, and Arnold Palmer glassware.

It occurred to me the only item not represented by Arnold Palmer Inc. was Arnold Palmer ink, but then I found deep at the bottom of the bag a fully functioning Arnold Palmer pen. There was even a customized ringtone with Palmer saying, "This is Arnold Palmer. Pick it up!"

The day was full of presentations about all the benefits of each of these aspects of Arnold Palmer Enterprises. The nights were swanky meals, drinks and included a pre-dinner address by the actual Arnold Palmer. I didn't take notes on what he said, but I recall how gracious and sincere his remarks were and how many of these mostly well-off attendees looked at him so adoringly.

And why not? Each had a personal connection to Palmer, however fleeting for some, and each was using his name to sustain their livelihoods. It was a powerful connection. I was mostly aloof. I had no connections, no one with whom to naturally mingle. The most significant personal introduction I enjoyed was when a distinguished, warm gentleman came up and introduced himself while I was sitting at the bar. I had no way of knowing it then, but the next dozen years would involve many joyful nights of laughter at that bar with that kind, gentle man. "Hi, I'm Jerry Palmer," he said. "Are you having a good time?"

After the morning sessions were concluding and I was lining up for free food, a necessary prelim for anyone about to engage in free golf, the man next to me was younger, probably in his late 20s. He turned to me with a warm smile, an extended hand, and said, "Hi! I'm Scott. I work for Arnold Palmer Enterprises."

This was the company founded by visionary agent/impressario Mark McCormack, who was famous for launching Palmer into promotional superstardom on the basis of a good-faith handshake deal that is still taught and admired in business schools. How consummate was Arnold Palmer Enterprises? Even Arnold Palmer was employed by Arnold Palmer Enterprises. So Scott had more considerable pull than, say, the Indiana gent who was there hawking Arnold Palmer dog collars.

He asked where I lived. I pointed out a nearby window and said, "If you look out that window, you can see where my dog crapped this morning."

"Man," he said, "you ought to be working for us!"

And just like that, I was. Within six weeks I'd be tasked with working with Doc to go through 15 legal-sized cardboard boxes that contained stacks of every newspaper and magazine clip that so much as mentioned Palmer's name. I soon found out the clips included everything from tournament victories from nearly 50 years before to slim paragraphs announcing Palmer would be addressing the local Boy Scouts at their annual gala.

This would become the interactive searchable timeline on www.ArnoldPalmer.com. The project would take more than two years and make me, coincidentally, an authority on Palmer facts and trivia whose base knowledge was exceeded only by my venerable friend, Doc. In fact, years later Palmer came up to me and asked, "How come you know more about me than I do?"

Chapter 3

It's Always a Heyday in Latrobe

It could happen at breakfast at Youngstown Grille or while fetching office donuts at Dainty Pastry Shoppe or stopping in for coffee and a gas-up at the Sheetz convenience mart. It's a small town where most everyone knows most everyone else. It's the informal kind of place where you're likely to hear hey more than hello. So before you sip your morning's first cup of coffee, you're likely to say hey to your kid's gym teacher, hey to the guy who fixes your furnace, or hey to the girl who waited on you the night before when you stopped in for pizza at the Hotel Loyal. In Latrobe, Pennsylvania, everyday is a heyday.

And on many occasions, you'd surprisingly say hey to Arnold Palmer. He was never cloistered, never reclusive, never circumspect. He wasn't some wax figure fastidious caretakers wheeled out for ceremonial duties. He was wholly present, engaged, and eager to meet both friends and strangers alike. And he was everywhere. "He was in here for breakfast every other week or so," said Scott Levin, owner of the Youngstown Grille. "He liked our French toast so much he asked for the recipe so he could have it made for him when he left for the winter. He'd have us deliver it to his home, and Jerry Palmer was always in here. He was just a great guy, too. We miss them both."

Levin remembers the time Arnold Palmer was in for breakfast when an awestruck young father sheepishly approached his table with his two-year old son in his arms. "He told him he'd named the boy Palmer in his honor," Levin said. "They'd never met before. It was beautiful, and it happened right here in the Youngstown Grille."

But small-town recognition wasn't guaranteed even in Youngstown even among global icons and one-time federal officials once charged with safe-guarding the nation. Levin said Palmer and Pennsylvania Governor and former Homeland Security Director Tom Ridge were once having breakfast. Both were wearing AriZona Iced Tea, the company that makes Arnold Palmer Teas, logo shirts. "My son saw the shirts," Levin said, "and asked if Palmer and Ridge were company sales reps." He was sort of correct. Palmer sold his rights for the drink to AriZona in 2006, and four years later, the company was reporting sales in excess of $100 million.

Latrobe named the local airport after Palmer in 1999 and put a larger-than-life Zenos Frudakis bronze statue of him across from the entrance in 2007. But the airport wasn't just a place where he was commemorated. The Arnold Palmer Regional Airport was also where Arnold Palmer also went to work.

From 1970 through 1984 and again from 1996 right up to his 2016 passing, he was a working member of the Westmoreland County Airport Authority. The post—one of nine—is a political appointment. Members serve at the pleasure of three county commissioners who serve at the pleasure of roughly 357,000 constituents. There's nothing ceremonial, nothing fun, about it. Appointees are expected to ensure flight departures/

arrivals run smoothly, snow removal gets accomplished in a timely manner, and that parking lot potholes are filled. There's nothing glamorous about the position.

But there was certainly some eye-popping glamour to the man occupying it. Gabe Monzo is the airport manager. He said locals were respectfully non-plussed, but Palmer's presence sometimes rattled guests there doing business with the airport authority. "Sometimes we'd get someone bidding on a contract," Monzo said, "and these were some pretty affluent people, and they'd get real nervous and stumble over their words. And he was hard of hearing so he'd really stare at whomever was speaking, and that only made them more nervous."

One time Palmer casually mentioned how some weeds at one of the airport properties were looking a bit shaggy. He wasn't mad, Monzo said, just making a casual observation. The next day the Associated Press ran a story saying the son of a greenskeeper was complaining airport grass needed cutting. "I got calls from reporters from all over the country," Monzo said. "He apologized and whenever he wanted to point something like that out again he was careful to do so when there weren't any reporters around."

What many people, who like to say they're a "people person," really mean is they're a "some people person." They like to confine their mingling to those who share certain refined characteristics. They'll shake hands if they're pretty certain the hands are clean—and even then they have a squirt of hand sanitizer ready to slay any germ that may have jumped hosts during contact. Palmer was truly a people person who seemed to revel more in meeting the common man, preferring their often raucous and bracing honesty to the gentle deferences of more polite social classes. "He would tolerate people you and I couldn't stand," said Doc Giffin, Palmer's personal assistant. "He truly enjoyed meeting all kinds of people and hearing their stories."

Why this seemed so is one for the psychologists to discern. Perhaps it was because this son of a greenskeeper always saw so much of himself in them. Perhaps it was because he realized making others feel good made him feel good. Or maybe it was just because he was raised to judge people on how they behaved, not how much they earned. Either way, he left an indelible mark on so many Latrobe neighbors not only because he was Arnold Palmer, but also because he was just a really swell guy.

Latrobe truly has a small-town feel. Barbara Antinori, the wife of renowned Latrobe barber Vince Antinori, saw Palmer in the Latrobe parking lot about 40 years ago when she was getting contact lenses. "I'd just gotten mine, and he said he was going in to get his," she said. "We talked for about 30 minutes right there in the parking lot. He was just a gem."

When it comes to Palmer stories, local bartender and fastener parts salesman Joe Holliday really hit the jackpot. Well, sort of. He and Palmer in 2008 had a handshake deal to split a fortune. He was in Giant Eagle, a local grocery store, when he saw Palmer and Bob Demangone, a St. Vincent College graduate who'd been with Palmer since '92 and was an Arnold Palmer Enterprises vice president. "Well, I know Bob, and at the time, my ex-wife was grooming Palmer's dog, Mulligan," Holliday said. "So I go up, shake his hand, and he's just as friendly as can be. We were standing there by the lottery ticket station, and he must think that's why I'm there because he asks if I want to go in on tickets with him. He says, 'Give me $20.' So I open my wallet and all I have is $20. So I empty my wallet and give my last dollar to Arnold Palmer, who at the time was worth, I think, more than half a billion bucks. He says, 'If we win, we'll split it.'"

Together they bought four $10 scratch-offs. They took turns

scratching. First ticket: nothing. Second ticket: nothing. Third ticket: nothing. Fourth ticket? Let's just say Holliday shelled out his last $20 for a great Palmer story, and those are all winners. "He gave me a big smile and said, 'You win some, you lose some!'" Holliday said. "I told him he's won a lot more than he's lost. He laughed."

Then there was July 3, 1980, when Tim Kozusko was amidst the throbbing herd at the starting line before the gun sounded at the annual Fourth of July 5K run. Like hundreds of others, he was just stretching and getting ready to race. "I looked up, and there was Arnold," he said. "He was all by himself. He was 50 at the time. He was just standing there like everyone else. I said hello and wished him luck making his time. He smiled real friendly and said, 'Same to you!' It was like he was just another guy out participating in the holiday community run." Kozusko shared another more recent Palmer siting. "We were having dinner at The Rainbow Inn in Youngstown," Kozusko said. "The waitress seats us and says, 'You're never going to believe who was just sitting right there in that chair…Arnold Palmer!' I tell you, just seeing Arnold Palmer out and about—it never got old."

Among treasured family photos, Diane Wilson still keeps a picture of Gary Player getting his hair cut. Her father-in-law was the late Art Wilson, the scissor man at the old XPX Barber Shop across the street from Holy Family Church. "Arnold used to come in all the time," she said. "Well, one day he comes in with Gary Player, says he's from South Africa and wants Art to give him his first flat top." She saw Palmer years later and introduced herself as his former barber's daughter-in-law. "'Oh, I really miss old Art,' he said. You could tell he really meant it," she said.

She has a signed picture of Palmer getting his hair cut, too. During his later years, Palmer had been getting his hair scissored at Gregory's Hair

Center across the State Route 981 from the Palmer airport. Customer Jim Beattie was there the day Palmer was celebrating his 86th birthday. He'd seen the news on *SportsCenter*. "I wished him Happy Birthday, and he said, 'Could we make it 39?'" Beattie said. "I said, 'Ah, I'll give you 2 strokes, and we'll make it 37.' He smiled and gave me a big thumbs-up. He loved the golf connection."

A year later, Beattie was playing a casual round at nearby Glengarry Golf Links the day Palmer pilot Pete Luster took Palmer's ashes on a ceremonial spin through the skies over Latrobe as a widely-viewed rainbow appeared over the town. The picture Beattie took is still heralded on the club's website.

Dave Carfang's father, Dick, and his Uncle Ed opened The Pond in 1954, and it was family owned through 2015 when the Carfangs sold it to Bill Wano. It was considered so representative of true Latrobe that in 2013 when Golf Channel was in town to film *Arnie*, the epic, three-part Palmer documentary, they didn't send their production crews to any of the fashionable Route 30 sports bars. They sent them to The Pond. The bar has a warm and colorful history. It's where Winnie used to get her hair styled. "The second floor is apartments, and we rented one of them to Mark Cialko, who for years used it for his hair salon," said Dick Carfang, who was 91 in 2017. "And every time she'd get her hair done, she'd take home a Pond pizza."

Palmer himself confirmed this to Dave Carfang during a 1996 visit arranged by Geano Agostino, Latrobe's Rolling Rock beer distributor at the time. "We were at the club, and Geano says, 'Let's go see if The King's in today,'" Dave said. "So we go in, and there he is in his workshop, tinkering with his clubs. Geano introduces me as an owner of The Pond, and he stops what he's doing, turns to me and says, 'My daughters were raised on Pond pizza.' Then he asks all these questions about how we're doing. It's a beautiful memory."

Dick keeps a memento of a 57-year-old memory folded in his wallet. It's from October 2, 1960. Less than four months after winning the U.S. Open, Palmer was honoring a commitment to play a pro-member tournament at the Latrobe Elks Golf Club. The other pros were all local, but one of the committed locals just happened to be Palmer. "My buddy, Wayne Bitner, was a member and he was having a beer before he went to the Elks for the blind draw," Dick said. "As he was leaving, he says, 'If I get Palmer, Dick, you're my caddie!' He came back later on, opens the door, and says, 'Hello, caddie!'"

So Dick Carfang will never forget the day so many years ago when he got an up-close hometown view of what all America was then enjoying: watching Palmer play golf.

Some Palmer stories aren't noteworthy for exactly what happened, but for how eager the storytellers are to share them. Raymond Robb's anecdote is one of them. It involves Palmer and some real foxes. And that's not slang for pretty women. No, the foxes Robb is discussing are genus *Vulpus*. "It was right in the field by the Route 30 cloverleaf between Latrobe and Youngstown," he said. "It was 1960. He'd just won the U.S. Open and was everywhere, really popular. Well, I see these foxes out in the field, a mother with two young ones. They're just playing. It's just me and this other guy watching when this car pulls up. The guy gets out, and across the street comes Arnold Palmer all by himself. And he just starts watching the foxes with us. The three of us stood there shooting the breeze and watching this family of foxes. We were there about 15 minutes, and he says, 'Well, I have to go.' He tells us to have a nice day. And that's my Arnold Palmer story."

Did Robb have any others? "Just from high school when he made the golf team and I didn't," he said. "I remember being disappointed but not too bad. He was a pretty good golfer."

Some stories, like Jim Ramsey's, come with a bit of a boast. Ramsey, who was 90 years old in 2017, claims he's the last living man to have witnessed Palmer win the Pennsylvania high school golf title. "It was 1946," he said. "The match was held at the Penn State course. Some of the ladies from the club asked me to drive them up to cheer him on. One of them had this old Buick. It wasn't like today's tournaments. We walked right with him the whole time. He was friendly as always. It was a lot of fun. What I remember most is how he saw this kid mowing these raised bunkers—kind of like the grass atop the church pews at Oakmont. Well, he notices the kid and right in the middle of what was then the biggest tournament of his life goes over and says, 'Hey, bud, that's not how you're supposed to mow those. Let me show you.' And he starts working the mower. He wasn't being pushy. He was just helping the kid out."

Ramsey remembers him still helping people out about 40 years later. His elderly uncle and aunt were members at the club and still enjoyed lunches there once a week. "My aunt was still driving, but by then my uncle had lost sight in both eyes. Getting around was a real struggle, but they really loved being at the club," Ramsey said. "On this day they couldn't find a close place to park. So they're hobbling across the lot, and Arnold sees them. He goes right up to my uncle and puts his arm around him and helps him walk. Then they get to his spot right near the front door. He turns to my aunt and says, 'From now on whenever you come here, this is your parking spot.' And for as long as they lived, it was. The spot he'd told them to park in was his."

The first time Steve Limani met Palmer he had to overcome years of instinctual training to keep from pulling his service revolver on him. Limani was a new Pennsylvania state trooper in 2006 when he

48

was ordered to run radar from his cruiser at a site where residents had been complaining about reckless speeders. The site? Legend's Lane off Arnold Palmer Drive.

Palmer's office had called to complain that motorists were violating the 35 mph speed limit on an obstructed turn where golf carts frequently crossed, and one of the occupants of those golf carts was Palmer. "I'm there one day, and these ominous clouds start rolling in, and it starts getting darker and darker," he said. "Finally, the skies just open up. Only the truly crazy people are out in this kind of storm, so I put down the radar gun, start filling out routine crash reports."

Then came a succession of loud quick bangs louder than thunder, and they were right on his driver's side window. Limani jumped. Had he been sipping hot coffee, he'd have scalded himself in places the Kevlar vests don't protect. "It was Mr. Palmer," Limani said, "and he was laughing like a little schoolgirl. He said, 'Good thing I didn't have a gun! I could have shot you!' I said, 'Well, I *do* have a gun, and you shouldn't be scaring me like that!"

It was the start of a decade-long friendship. Palmer has said anyone who has a bodyguard probably needs a bodyguard. (He was being dismissive of the concept. He never had one because he never needed one and thought that those that have them usually needed them because they're jerks.) Nonetheless, that's the day Limani became his defacto personal security detail. He'd escort him to public events, assist in traffic considerations, and just hang out and learn how to treat people, something that became an actual job requirement when he was elevated to community service officer. "I learned from watching him that the most important person in the world was the person right in front of him," Limani said. "When he was in public, I'd just stand back and marvel at the grace with which he'd conduct himself. Oh, how I looked up to that man."

There is one place that enlistees in Arnie's Army might be surprised to see their leader.

"I was sitting in there getting my nails done in spring 2016 and in walks Arnold Palmer," said a friend who asked not to be named, I guess, out of fear of violating some obscure toenail code. "He sat down, said hello, and proceeded to get a pedicure. When I was leaving, he'd finished and was on his way to get a manicure. They said he came in all the time."

Arnie's Army has GIs all over the world, but Palmer's true foot soldiers are all in Latrobe.

Roots

Anita Manoli knew Palmer for 83 years. She met him when she was four years old, and Doris Palmer invited the neighbors over for cake. It was Mrs. Palmer's son's fifth birthday. "We lived on the other side of the creek," she said. "I remember Doris coming over and asking my mother if she wanted to bring us kids over for cake. We've been friends ever since."

Life-long friends, in fact. She last visited Palmer in his office in June 2016, three months prior to his passing. "We talked about all the old times," she said, "so many happy memories."

The two neighbors were friends and youthful confidants who shared with one another their dreams of the future. "He always knew he was going to be something special," she said. "In his case it wasn't ego. It was prophesy. He was always thinking in terms of who he was going to be. From a very young age, he always knew he was going to be—not just a golfer—but someone special."

Palmer was aware of the importance of branding essentials before he'd even been old enough to drive. The boy, who would go on to sign what some guess might be more than a million autographs, was signing them before anyone was even asking for them. Manoli remembers seeing him sign his name, "Arny," not "Arnie." She asked what he was doing. "He said, 'I'm trying to see which one will look better when I become a professional golfer.' He revered Bob Jones and even as a young boy he knew he was the one to emulate."

Some of those close to Palmer doubted Manoli's claim that he ever spelled his name as anything other than "Arnie." They said she must be misremembering, but she has insisted she was correct all her life and she has proof.

She still has her 1946 Latrobe Senior High School yearbook. In still recognizable penmanship that would one day become nearly as famous as the man wielding the pen, it is signed, "Arny Palmer." "I told him 'Arny' looked all wrong," she says. "I said, 'You need to spell it 'Arnie.'" Sure, it's anecdotally factual, but she has even more concrete proof on a framed page from the next year's yearbook. Beside Palmer's senior Class of '47 picture is a clean-looking Palmer signature beneath an inscription that thoughtfully says, "To the girl who always gives me all my advice and one of my best friends. I will always remember you."

And he always did. "We were such good friends," said Manoli, who taught Spanish at nearby Derry schools and at St. Vincent before retiring in 1993. A daughter of a local stone cutter/monuments maker, she said her friend—the relationship never turned romantic—wasn't the first famous Palmer in Latrobe. "His father, Deacon, was a celebrity before Arnold," she says. "Even during the Depression, golf was a big deal in Latrobe, and anybody who gave golf lessons to Fred Rogers and all the other children of the local muckety-mucks was a big deal. And everyone

Arnold Palmer, left, plays a different kind of green with his father, Deacon Palmer, at Arnold's Latrobe, Pennsylvania, home in 1964. (AP *Images*)

knew how much Deke cared for people."

If one of his caddies was having a problem, Deacon, who basically ran the whole shebang at Latrobe Country Club, not only knew about it, but also took steps to solve it. She remembers hearing the story of young Martin Borza complaining of a toothache and being in obvious pain. "When Deke found out, he told him to go see Dr. Wright, a local dentist and club member," she said. "It got taken care of."

It's an example of how everyone pitched in during tough times and how Latrobe worked.

"It was a small town where everyone helped one another," she said. "And Deke and Doris Palmer were beloved."

They were so beloved that it became local fodder for the town gossips when the lovebirds had younger Palmer siblings, Jerry and later Sandy, 15 years after Arnold was born: "Everyone in town was saying, 'What in the world is going on with Deke and Doris?'"

By then, her friend was already barnstorming western Pennsylvania, winning individual and team awards for his rising golf skills. Yearbook team pictures uniformly show Palmer smiling and the eyes of his teammates all riveted on him and what he was saying. Most of his teammates were from families that belonged to the country club, but it was the greenskeeper's son who had all the magnetism. Manoli says the whole family had what she calls a "quiet charisma," one that inspired without ever verging on braggadocio, and also an incredible work ethic.

Palmer used those admirable qualities to excel at another pastime. "Back then, when we were in high school," she said, "we had long lunches built into each day. We'd play outside, eat, and socialize. But Arnie spent his lunch hours playing pool down at the old Plaza Hotel. He became one of the best billiard players in town. It just came naturally to him. Everything did."

Indeed, Palmer was a 17-year-old golf sensation when he won the western Pennsylvania qualifier to play in the annual Hearst Junior National Amateur Golf Tournament. He sent Manoli a letter describing all that transpired. She still has it. "Here he was in Hollywood, this 17-year-old kid from Latrobe and he took time to write his neighbor. He mentioned very matter-of-factly three things that happened. He said he'd had an arranged date with what he described as a young 'ingénue,' that he went swimming in Esther Williams' pool, and that he played golf with Clark Gable. He wasn't bragging and he never ever lied or exaggerated."

The trip was pivotal, too, because at the Hearst he met and befriended fellow competitor Buddy Worsham, who persuaded Palmer to attend Wake Forest with him. Manoli is adamant that she was never surprised that the boy, who once toyed with calling himself "Arny Palmer," became the man known and loved around the world as Arnold Palmer. "We all knew he was special," she says. "I don't think you'd find a person alive who would have said, 'Oh, that Palmer kid will never amount to anything.' It was the exact opposite."

So how much of a role does Latrobe, that old steel town, have to do with him becoming who he became? "It was essential," Manoli said. "His parents, his family, and this town gave him all the tools he needed to become so beloved and so successful. The key, too, was that he never left…If he hadn't always come back to Latrobe, if he'd have moved on, no one would have ever heard of him. He'd have become just another golfer. Instead he lived and died in Latrobe and became Arnold Palmer, a man the world will never forget."

Chapter 4

Jim Nantz

Jim Nantz recalled his first visit to Latrobe, Pennsylvania, with sartorial precision. The King was looking more ratty than regal. And he was engaged in one of those mundane tasks that would seem far beneath the dignity of such a celebrated persona. "He was wearing these black sweatpants and an old yellow sweatshirt," Nantz said of the Pittsburgh Steelers colors Palmer was sporting. "And he was walking his dog…I saw that and thought, *So this is what you get when you find Arnold Palmer at home in Latrobe.* I've never known a man so comfortable in his own skin."

It was June 13, 1994, a date of relevance for multiple reasons to Nantz and anyone who cares about American sports. Palmer was 64 and would later that day be driving an hour west down the Pennsylvania Turnpike to enjoy a practice round at historic Oakmont Country Club where he would be playing in his final U.S. Open.

It was also significant because news was sweeping the country that the wife of NFL/pop culture icon O.J. Simpson, Nicole Brown Simpson, and Ron Goldman were brutally slain outside her Brentwood, California, home. The week would end with Palmer giving a tear-filled farewell press conference in the Oakmont media tent while televisions in the next room began broadcasting the police chase of the man who once starred with Palmer in a chummy series of popular Hertz rent-a-car ads.

Nantz said the week's cascade of memories remain indelible. "I was hosting a dinner at Oakmont inside the club for Rolex," he says. "Arnold's a longtime Rolex ambassador and so am I. So was tennis great Vitas Gerulaitis. After the dinner Arnold comes up and asks if we'd like

CBS announcer Jim Nantz, who delivered a moving speech at Arnold Palmer's funeral, was a longtime confidant of Arnold Palmer. *(Howdy Giles)*

to see Latrobe. 'I'd love to show you around,' he said. So Vitas and I jump at the chance. And the next morning at 7:00 AM, there's a car outside waiting to take me and Vitas to Latrobe and Arnold Palmer."

It was the start of a real friendship and the first of dozens of trips Nantz would make to Latrobe. If CBS was broadcasting a marquee NFL game involving the Steelers at Heinz Field, Nantz made sure to build in time to visit Latrobe. "He was just so proud of Latrobe. That town and those people just kept him so grounded," Nantz said. "He never forgot who he was and where he came from. Latrobe, that old steel town, is the crucible that forged Arnold Palmer."

He and Vitas got the grand tour that day from the most informed tour guide. They saw the office, the workshop, the warehouse, the club. "I remember him showing us where they'd scattered the ashes of his parents at the club. He said, 'Someday, I'll be right there with them.' I said, 'Arnold, you're never going to die.' I really believed that," Nantz said.

The famed announcer was always surprised by how a man as famous and beloved as Palmer could, if he chose, be left to himself in Latrobe. "In Latrobe, he was just such a regular guy," he said. "It's just so unique to today's sports celebrity culture."

Most every celebrity athlete or golfer today, Nantz says, is surrounded by agents, nutritionists, swing coaches, trainers—a regal retinue of paid hangers-on who spend their appointed face time doing suck-up things that'll justify their continued existence on the payroll.

"And I get it," he said. "There's a lot of money involved and there's a lot of pressure on celebrities to perform. But Arnold was the total opposite. It was just him and anywhere he went, but especially in Latrobe, there was no buffer between him and the people that wanted to meet him."

Nantz noted that Palmer didn't reside in a gated community. He lived in a neighborhood. His office and residence were located on Legends Lane, an unimposing little cul-de-sac that today features four homes and the Palmer office and workshop. Its front door is crowned by the iconic red, yellow, white, and green umbrella.

The home Nantz saw in 1994 was the one Arnold and Winnie Palmer paid $17,000 in cash for in 1955 and was his home until 2006, when he and his new bride, Kit, built another home just up the hill. They're nice homes, sure, but if you were searching for the home of a world-famous multi-millionaire golfer, you'd pass these homes right by. There's no gilt. No dazzle. And especially there's no perimeter. No security. No fence. No guard dogs. There was just Arnold and Winnie. "I couldn't believe it," Nantz said. "There wasn't even a little gate, not even one of those generic little 'No Trespassing' signs. Anyone could just walk up the street and just knock on his door. I said this to him, and he said, 'Oh, that happens.'"

Nantz asked what he'd do when it did. Palmer said he answered the door. "He said it was usually just someone who wanted a picture or an autograph," Nantz said. "He'd greet them and give them what they were there for. He said they were always very courteous and appreciative."

Nantz's tour and chat with Palmer was very relaxed and unhurried as if the legendary golfer had cleared his schedule just to spend the day with them. So it's helpful to understand, too, what else Palmer had going on this day. He had interviews, meetings, and a U.S. Open practice round at Oakmont ahead of him. The entire golf world would have its eyes on him, and a big part of Palmer believed not only could he still make the cut but he could maybe—maybe—win the whole damn thing.

About this and other recollections, Nantz and Gerulaitis were marveling as they left that day and returned to Oakmont. "We were just basking in the glow," he says. "We felt blessed. Vitas said it had been one of the best days of his life."

Cruelly, Gerulaitis' life sample was about to conclude. The popular tennis champion was found dead just 90 days later. He'd been sleeping at a friend's Southampton, Long Island, guest home when an improperly installed pool heater caused gas to seep into the bedroom where Gerulaitis was sleeping. His death was due to carbon monoxide poisoning. He was 40.

So some of Nantz's Latrobe memories mingle euphoria with poignancy, especially after the September 25, 2016, death of his friend, Palmer. "I'm still grieving," he says. "I think I always will. I told him how much I loved him every time we talked. I just feel so blessed to have been an up close witness to such an example of such grace. Arnold Palmer was a living, breathing example of human grace."

What would Nantz, the epitome of timely eloquence, say to Palmer if he could talk to him just one more time? "Thank you," he said, "just the thought of trying to summarize all that man meant to me and the world overwhelms."

Chapter 5

Palmer's Letters and Caddies

The wistful tone in our cheerful postmistress' voice caught me by surprise, but it was plainly evident. She was missing the daily deluge of mail that would flood into the otherwise nondescript P.O. Box 52 in the Youngstown, Pennsylvania, post office. "Yeah, getting all those Arnold Palmer letters and all those Arnold Palmer packages from all over the world made the day more interesting," she said.

Interesting, all right. And relentless. "The letters started coming in right after his first Masters victory in 1958," said Doc Giffin, Palmer's personal assistant. "By the time I got there in '66, it was already pretty heavy. The more interesting thing to me is how it never diminished. Right up to his passing, we were getting between 15 to 20 letters each and every day."

Each was acknowledged. None were ignored. And none were ever charged even a penny in return postage. The phenomenon was noticed by reporters from *The Beaches Leader* in Jacksonville, Florida, who in 1988 interviewed Giffin about Palmer's mail. He said then: "It would

Arnold Palmer, who always made sure to take care of his caddies, hangs out with his 15-year-old caddie, Jack Wallace, during the 1965 National Open. (AP *Images*)

be easier to weigh his mail than count it. For instance, he gets about 3,000 picture requests every year. Every day, we get four or five charity auction requests for a contribution. If we'd have given away a club for every charity requesting one, we would have run out of clubs about 20 years ago. As he changes gloves, he saves them and signs them. Each one brings a charity about $100. We figured up the other day just how many autographs he's signed. It's over a million. Think about how long that would take a person."

He had a million autographs by 1988 and still had 28 years of signing left. John Hancock had nothing on Arnold Palmer, who would often enter the office before his staff and begin to tackle the stack by his desk. He'd spend up to three hours signing photo after photo in that impeccable penmanship, and the photos would be destined for mailboxes around the world. He knew if he'd take even a day off the stack would be twice as high the next morning.

Think of the dedication to the task, the reciprocal devotion to the fans. Think of nearly six decades of signing your name. And Palmer always tried to personalize each photo and add a cheery salutation. Other aging golfers got backaches. Palmer would get writer's cramp. Giffin remembers seeing him shaking his hand to fend off the numbness, then immediately resuming the task.

More than half of those reaching out sought autographed pictures destined for framed prominence above mantels or on walls in game rooms, pro shops, or restaurants around the world. Many of the letters were from people who'd been inspired by Palmer. Some were proposing business partnerships. Some would send him shirts or other gestures of gratitude, a way of reaching out to let an icon know he'd somehow touched them.

Some of the packages were more unusual. It wasn't uncommon for the Youngstown post office to receive oblong boxes that inside had the carefully wrapped golf equivalent of divining rods. There were putters, more than 2,000 of them. They take up an entire wall inside Palmer's office workshop. Resting in a spider web of wires that other connoisseurs might use to store fine wines, the wall of putters never failed to enthrall visitors. Then there's the odd assortment of fat ones, skinny ones, ones that look like they could hammer rocks. Green putters, bottle putters, putters wearing protective black socks. Yes, it's like the Armour hot dog jingle right down to one reddish weiner putter.

And with every single thing that came in, a signature went out. That includes farm equipment. "One gentleman some years back showed up at the office with a tractor that was the same model as the one Arnold used in the Pennzoil commercials," Giffin said. "He wanted him to sign it. He did, of course. He never said no."

And many of the letters were ones initiated by Palmer. He'd send congratulatory letters to PGA, LPGA, and Champion tour winners. He'd read the local papers and would write letters to encourage those who were struggling or cheer those who were succeeding. More than any athlete, he understood the permanence and power of writing and mailing real letters to people who yearn for inspiration. Even a well-worded email eventually gets deleted when its generic charms dissipate. Actual letters, like many of the ones Palmer penned, wind up in family bibles that get passed down for generations.

It was like that with Brandt Snedeker. After Palmer's death, he told *Golfweek* that he spent a soulful evening relishing the 15 letters Palmer had written to him when he wasn't yet established on the PGA Tour. "I'm there looking at all the stuff that he had sent me and thinking about the time he spent on me...I was a no-name guy when he started writing me letters and I realize he's done that for a countless number of people,"

Snedeker said. "It kind of hit me the time he put into everybody else but himself. That's going to be something you can't replace."

Palmer would dictate the letters and sign the printed results. No one knows how much all that time and postage cost Palmer. Some estimates say it was more than $100,000 in postage a year. No wonder the local postmistress lamented the end of so much revenue.

You have to think, too, of the time. Would Palmer have won more golf tournaments if he'd have instead used all his signing time to perfect his putting stroke? But he obviously believed it was more important to respond to the million or so gestures from friends or strangers who just wanted to thank him, to support him, or just show how much they cared. Clearly, the feeling was mutual.

****

By 2010 my answer to the question if I knew Arnold Palmer had become far more satisfying—both to the questioner and me personally. Did I know Arnold Palmer? "Not only do I know him," I'd say, "we're friends." (This was about a year before it dawned on me that Arnold Palmer was everyone's friend.)

I think our relationship began to ease into true friendship when I realized his guard was totally down during our talks. These were mostly Q & As for his *Kingdom Magazine*. Editors would forward a list of maybe 30 questions geared toward features in the upcoming issue. So a sprinkling of questions might be about high-performance vehicles, fashion, a rising PGA star, or an upcoming major.

At first I used to pretty much stick to the script, but then I began deviating. Our talks became more freewheeling, more engaging, more zesty. Yet, part of me was still cowed by his image. I mean, here I was bantering with Arnold Palmer. Didn't I need to maintain a certain professional demeanor? I thought I did. I always dressed immaculately and made sure all the necessary grooming—haircut, mustache trimmed, etc.—had been fulfilled. And without fail, I'd extend a firm introductory handshake and respectful salutation. I'd say something like: "Good morning, Mr. Palmer! I can't tell you how much I look forward to these sessions and to hearing your insights."

He cocked his head and gave me a wry look and then said the words that let me know just how much our relationship had changed: "And I can't tell you how much I enjoy having you come in here to blow so much sweet smoke up my ass!"

And together we roared with laughter. I'd still consider myself a trivial intimate, but I now knew I could talk to him as an equal—a Latrobe equal—someone comfortable telling ribald jokes and sassy insults. In the parlance of western Pennsylvania, Palmer and I could jag each other.

I knew right then just how well this wealthy and beloved icon would fit in with all the profane jokers I hung with at The Pond. They're loud, brash, opinionated, and prone to uproarious laughter when exposed to frequent bursts of lightning wit from either owner/raconteur Dave Carfang or from one another. Pond regulars included farmers, businessmen, steel workers, quarry men, lawyers, reporters, teachers, coaches, and cops.

It's the kind of boisterous small-town dynamic where I believed Deacon Palmer would have felt right at home.

So would his son.

So, of course, right after I left Palmer's office, I hustled down to The Pond to tell Dave and the gang all about Palmer's self-deprecating sarcastic comments. They loved it. A few of them knew Palmer, too, and we all started telling our favorite stories. In Latrobe, Pennsylvania, at least in those days, many of the conversations eventually led back to Palmer. I later that day returned to my office to transcribe our conversation, part of which centered on Palmer's stated discomfort over being the bronze subject of yet another tribute statue. This one was at his Wake Forest alma mater. But before I did that, I felt moved to compose the first true fan letter I'd written in more than 40 years.

Dear Mr. Palmer,

During our most recent Kingdom interview, you humbly mentioned how accolades have a way of making you uncomfortable. Well, brace yourself, this is going to be mighty unpleasant.

Being able to interview you so many times over the last 10 years has been one of the most personally enriching experiences of my professional life. My dear father died in 2004, but he lives on with me, especially every time I walk into your office. I know how proud he'd be that his son has so many frequent opportunities to banter with his hero.

Here's a secret: I've learned to always leave my recorder playing a minute or so after our interview concludes. That way I have audio record of you saying great things about me like, "You always do a superb job here," and "I love the way you work." One day I intend to stitch all the wonderful things you've said about me and play them in order on my phone greeting right after the introductory message, "You've reached Chris Rodell. Here are four minutes of Arnold Palmer saying nice things about me. Have a great day!"

And thank you, especially, for the wonderful staff you've assembled. To be friends with Debbie, Gina, Bob, Cori, and Doc, especially, has been one of my life's blessings.

So thank you for always welcoming me into your world. It's a thrill every time I get to sneak in under the ropes. And if you're embarrassed by the statue they've built for you at Wake Forest, wait until you get a load of the one me and the boys down at The Pond are going to build.

I swear, they're going to need to re-route all the inbound planes.

Warm regards,

Chris Rodell

Uncharacteristically, he did not respond with a letter of his own. Maybe he knew it'd be unnecessary. Maybe personally responding to such praise, like another statue, made him feel uncomfortable. Either way, I was not at all miffed. Like so many other foot soldiers in Arnie's Army, I just felt compelled to let him know how much he meant to me.

Little did I know at the time, he was about to sign his illustrious name beneath a letter that would exert far more meaning in my life than a common courtesy thank you note.

****

Recipients of Palmer's letters were often the caddies. Palmer used the power of the pen to put on them the track of career success.

You'd never guess from the pictures of the young men back then that the lads were destined to become leaders, captains of industry, pillars of their communities. In fact, looking back over more than 30 years, one of them had a somewhat facetious description of himself and his associates. "Man, we were all just a bunch of goofballs," said Ed Myers, who started caddying at Latrobe Country Club when he was 14.

But Palmer looked at each of them and saw something besides goofballs. He saw potential. "He saw it as his duty to help caddies get into good schools and get them jobs," Myers said. "He did it for me. He did it for my friends, and I'm sure he did it for others throughout his entire life. He was perfectly happy to have his name used to help others."

It could have been as simple as suggesting a young man or woman put the name Arnold Palmer under the references on the resume. That's how it happened with Myers. He had caddied on and off for nine years since he was in the eighth grade. He wasn't Palmer's regular club caddie during those years but became his go-to guy in 1983 after graduating from Penn State with a degree in civil engineering. "The economy was still pretty tough recovering from the recession in the late 1970s," he said. "After graduation I worked pretty hard trying to find a job in my field. I was not at all concerned about location and really hoped to move out west somewhere, but I knew that I would move to wherever I ended up finding a job. So I was back at the club when his regular caddie went back to school."

Myers said Palmer wondered why the recent graduate with the prestigious degree was still humping clubs, forgetting how many CEOs and captains of industry would chuck it all to carry his bag for just one day. He explained his situation, and Palmer offered his name as a reference. "This turned things around immediately," Myers said. "All of a sudden, I started getting calls for interviews. I ended up getting interviews from two firms in Baltimore, both of which ended up offering me a job. Both of the interviewees were intrigued by the Arnold Palmer reference. Before I started my interview with my eventual employer, he announced that the guy who used Arnold Palmer as a reference was in the office, and everyone naturally came out of their offices or cubicles to greet me. As it turns out, my future boss was a huge golfer. In addition to being a pretty good golfer, he was also a student of the game and a minor golf historian. Of the two-hour interview, I would conservatively say we talked 60 minutes about golf and much of that about Mr. Palmer. My former boss actually retired from the engineering business and wound up being the executive director of the Maryland State Golf Association, so the Palmer reference helped far more than I could have imagined at the time."

Myers, who was age 56 in 2017, is now a senior principal at Kittelson & Associates in Baltimore. He has signed pictures of him and Palmer in his office. He doesn't foresee a day when the pictures don't draw smiles and questions. "His kind of popularity will never die," he said. "Arnold Palmer was one of a kind, and I'm not sure we'll see another like him."

Jeff Messich has no idea what happened to the 1985 letter that changed his life and the lives of six friends. No, it wasn't addressed to him, but it was all about him. It was from Palmer telling a Pennzoil executive that Messich would be a wise hire. His instincts must have been sound because 30 years later Messich is still with the company. So are two of his fellow Latrobe caddies that Messich helped get hired after he was brought on.

It's all worked out pretty well, so Messich wishes he could have the letter as a keepsake.

One problem: the letter recipient kept it for himself. "It had Arnold Palmer's signature on it, so he wasn't giving it away," he said. "I'd love to have it, sure, because that's the letter that made my whole career. And it was all thanks to Arnold Palmer."

Messich caddied at Latrobe Country Club from 1979 through 1983 and probably did so 100 times for Palmer. He was such a caddieshack staple that when his future employer filmed one of its popular motor oil commercials at the club it cast Messich in a starring role. Well, part of him, at least. "Yeah, I thought I was going to have a bigger role," Messich said. "I was really excited, but when the commercial aired all of Messich that was visible was my arm."

The morning shoots always involved afternoon rounds of golf. Messich caddied for one of the head executives and asked how he could land a sales position after graduating from Clarion University in spring of '83. He was given a number to call after the Christmas holiday. That call led to another circling of a calendar date after his spring break. "They wanted me for an interview in Fairview, New Jersey, in three days," Messich said. "I knew what I had to do: call Doc Giffin. I knew he could get me a letter of recommendation from Arnold Palmer."

He did, and the letter sparkled. Palmer said Messich was a hard-working and dedicated leader who'd be an asset to the company, likely echoing what three decades of Pennzoil performance evaluators would say. "They couldn't believe I had a letter of personal reference from Arnold Palmer," Messich said. "I knew right away I could miserably fail that interview, and it was a cinch I'd get the job. So, yeah, I owe my whole career to a letter from Arnold Palmer."

And Pennzoil got more than an able and affable salesman when it got Messich. It also got a reliable fountain of entertaining stories anytime anyone asked, "So, do you have any good Arnold Palmer stories?" Here are two.

Messich was a tight end/defensive end for the Latrobe Senior High Wildcats. He told Palmer the team was coming together, becoming a real dynamo. He said Palmer should catch one of the Friday night games down at Memorial Stadium. "He said it had been ages since he'd been to a game," Messich said, "and it sounded like a good idea."

Shortly after the next home game against the rival Mount Pleasant Senior High Vikings, word started to spread to the field that Palmer was in attendance. The inspirational news fired up the Wildcats. *Palmer was watching! Their greatness would be witnessed by a legend!* But it was not to be. The team laid an egg. In fact, both teams did. Goose eggs, really.

Final score: Latrobe 0, Mt. Pleasant 0. "I asked him the next day what he thought," Messich said. "He said, 'I think the Latrobe band should have been on the field, and the team should have been in the stands.'"

Another time, Messich was beside Palmer on a Monday afternoon when things were so slow it was like they had the course to themselves. Palmer drilled a drive over the crest of the par-4, 17th hole. As soon as they topped the hill, they were surprised to see the green ringed four deep with busloads of Japanese tourists. "He looked at me and asked if I knew what was going on," Messich said. "I told him I did not. He looked at me like, 'Boy, this is strange.' I just handed him his pitching wedge."

About 80 yards out, Palmer settled into his stance, drew the club back, and hit a high-arcing pitch right at the flag. Messich said, "It bounced once and went straight in the cup. The galley went nuts. He winked at me and says, 'What do you think they think of me now?'"

Some old caddies didn't get jobs, but they received indelible memories of strolling the fairways with a legend, and they're satisfied with those. Bill Bush will never forget the gravity-defying trajectory of a well-struck drive by Palmer, who was nearing his rugged prime. Bush was caddying for him at Latrobe in 1957 and remembers hearing stories of Deacon Palmer admonishing his son, "Just hit it as hard as you can. You'll figure out how to straighten it out later, but hit it hard, boy."

Bush, who was 15, said that primal lesson resulted in Palmer getting the ball to fly like it was afraid of getting another spanking. "He'd hit it so hard," he said, "the ball would get this crazy overspin that would make it scream out really low and fast. Then about 150 yards out, it would just shoot up like a rocket."

Like many Latrobe caddies of the time, Bush remembered Palmer's routine practice sessions. "We'd go out to some isolated hole, and [he'd] tell us to start heading down the fairway," he said. "You'd get maybe 120 yards out, and he'd yell to stop and drop the shag bag. Then you'd stand aside, and he'd just start hitting ball after ball. Every once in a while, one would go a little funny, but most of them would land right next to the bag."

After a while, Palmer would tell Bush to back up to vary the distance. Bush once lost sight of a ball and couldn't find it. He thought it was gone for good. Later that day during an actual round, Palmer hit an approach shot on the hole where they'd been shagging balls. "Before he headed to the green, he walked straight to where I'd lost that one ball. He takes his wedge and with one hand chops straight down," Bush said. "Up pops this ball. He catches it with his other hand, flips it to me, and said, 'And here's the one you missed.' I felt about two inches tall. He wasn't mad, but he didn't miss a thing. It just shows his level of concentration."

No one would confuse Bill Clark as a youthful goofball caddie. To him, caddying was more a calling than a job, something he felt in his bones. Part of it comes from where he went to work: Laurel Valley. The 53-year-old Clark has been caddying there 30 years, and if his legs will hold out, he'll do it for another 30. He loves the scenery, the challenge, and how no two rounds are ever the same. Laurel's clientele is pure posh. He's carried for Mario Lemieux, Bill Cowher, Lou Holtz, Charles Barkley, and Jim Boeheim.

The pros who've played it say it rivals any top tour course in beauty and degree of difficulty. So, yeah, Laurel is special. "Being there is to me like having an addiction," Clark said. "I get there and I don't want to leave. It feels like my second home."

The only thing that could make it any more special was when Palmer pulled up the driveway. "He had a way of mesmerizing everyone at Laurel just by being there," Clark said. "Everyone stopped and looked when he'd hit those drives."

Clark was tabbed to caddie for Palmer about 10 times. The feeling was always the same. "Surreal. I'd be walking up the fairways thinking, *I'm out here handing clubs to a legend.* I am one of those guys who grew up idolizing him," Clark said. "You could learn so much about humanity just by watching him. He always had time for everyone. There aren't many like that left. Now, it's all, 'So what can you do for me?'"

Clark's last loop with Palmer lasted just two holes when lightning cracked the horizon.

"He saw that and said, 'Okay, sorry, but we're done.' He was a lightning fanatic on the golf course," Clark said. "I couldn't believe my luck. I was so bummed."

Palmer paid all the caddies, Clark noted, the full fee with tip as if they'd completed the round. But he can't help but think about all he lost by missing those remaining 16 holes with Palmer. "We all knew just how special it was to have a man that wonderful, that rare, in our lives," he said. "But when he's gone, you wonder if it ever really happened. It's like a man like Arnold Palmer was some kind of dream."

Similarly, the golf coach at High Point University in North Carolina had trouble believing Palmer sent a personal letter on behalf of standout Latrobe golfer Ben Gjebre. "He was like, 'How the hell did you get this?" Gjebre said.

That former coach, J.B. White, said Palmer's referral definitely had an impact on his decision to offer Gjebre a spot on the team. "Who in their right mind wouldn't pay attention to a letter like that coming from Arnold Palmer?" White said. "And he was right on about Ben. I don't for a minute regret keeping Ben."

Gjebre keeps the letter framed in his bedroom. The letter reads:

I am pleased to write this letter of recommendation for Benjamin Gjebre, suggesting that he receive serious consideration as a student and potential member of a collegiate golf team.

While I have only been acquainted with Ben and his parents for a relatively short time as members at my Latrobe Country Club in Western Pennsylvania, I have had the opportunity to watch him play. He was No. 1 on this year's high school team that brought my alma mater its first ever state team golf championship just a few days after he won the individual championship of the Western Pennsylvania Athletic League as I did many years ago.

He is a personable young man of obvious talent who should do well in college ranks, not only as a golfer but, judging from his high school grades, as a student as well. I am impressed that his educational goal is to pursue an MBA degree.

Sincerely,
Arnold Palmer

Palmer may have felt a unique bond with Gjebre, who as of 2017 was a 25-year-old information technology sales rep with CDW in Phoenix. He won the 2009 Western Pennsylvania Interscholastic Athletic League previously won by Palmer in 1946–47. And with his Latrobe Senior High teammates, Gjebre helped win the state title.

One of his teammates that storied year was Palmer's grandson Will Wears. So Palmer was always there encouraging, teaching, counseling. "We were playing Glengarry [Golf Links, four miles from Latrobe Country Club], and a guy sees our Latrobe golf bags and asks if we ever saw Arnold Palmer," Gjebre said. "Will grinned and said, 'Oh, he's around.' And he was—always."

Gjebre grew up hearing of Palmer and realizing he was significant but had a youthful misunderstanding of the scope of the magnitude. That's just the way it is for kids in Latrobe. What's familiar becomes taken for granted. But an appreciation begins to accumulate, especially for high school golfers who practice daily at Latrobe Country Club, a literal monument to a legend who happens to be local. "You'd see him following us along in his cart with the two big Callaway bags filled with clubs," he said. "I remember seeing that cart sitting between the 3rd green and 4th tee. Driving was Arnold Palmer, and in the seat next to him was Jim Nantz."

Gjebre considers himself fortunate that awareness dawned when it really meant something. He became emotional when he told the next part of his story. "I was in the Grille Room getting ice for my drink and I look up and see I'm two feet from Arnold Palmer. He asks me, 'So what are you going to shoot today?' I said, 'I'm thinking I'm going to get nine pars.' He smiles and says, 'Nine pars? I want to see you birdie 'em all!'"

Gjebre will forever treasure the gold ball marker with umbrella insignia and pin Palmer personally presented him. But the best memory might have been the one Palmer initiated when he wasn't even in the room but rather was nearly 1,000 miles away. "Our championship banquet was at the country club," he said. "He took the time to call from Bay Hill to congratulate us. It was on the speaker phone, and everyone heard every word. Everyone who heard him got choked up. It's something I'll never forget."

Maybe that's why Gjebre doesn't carry his magnificent Palmer letter folded up in his pocket wherever he goes. Memories like that never fade or wrinkle.

Palmer at least once offered to write a letter that had life-saving potential. That's what happened with Dennis Charlesworth in 1973. He'd been hired to run Latrobe Country Club's tennis facility. He'd been a top player upon graduating from Indiana University of Pennsylvania in nearby Indiana, the birthplace of another Pennsylvania icon, actor Jimmy Stewart.

Palmer rarely played tennis and when he did was rarely serious. Charlesworth recalled the time Palmer came running onto the court barefoot, a clear violation of the court regulations approved by Palmer himself. The lawlessness put Charlesworth in an awkward position. "I said, 'You know, don't you, that you're not allowed to play without the proper footwear?' And, he said, 'And do you know who signs your checks?'" Charlesworth said.

The world was Palmer's kingdom, but Latrobe would always be his playground. Palmer was sufficiently impressed with Charlesworth that he asked him after one season if he'd be interested in committing to teach tennis at Bay Hill, Florida, during the winter months. "I thanked him but told him I was committed to serving in the Army. He said, 'I can get you out of that.' But I'd already made my decision," Charlesworth said.

An ROTC graduate, Charlesworth was assigned to the 82nd Airborne at Fort Campbell in Clarksville, Kentucky. The unit had suffered grievously in Vietnam and was in a re-grouping phase. Charlesworth was never sent overseas. He did end up requesting Palmer write him another letter. This one would be to the admission board at the school of business administration at the University of Alabama. He spent a career in human relations and today hands out business cards that tout he's a "Self-Appointed, Unofficial & International Ambassador of Latrobe, Pennsylvania."

He named his dog Arnie, too. A Schnauzer rescue dog, Arnie is a "real ladies man who loves to visit schools, nursing homes, and other people-friendly venues. I enjoy explaining the reason for his name. It's a great ice-breaker and opens many topics for Latrobe-related discussions," Charlesworth said. That inevitably leads to stories of the Schnauzer's namesake. "People are still always asking me to tell them Arnold Palmer stories. They all want to know what he's really like. I tell them all he's just as down-home as you can imagine."

And he's also patient and understanding. Palmer taught Patrick McGarrity that indelible lesson. McGarrity, who was 46 in 2017, did something in 1987 that might have earned a solid berating from men less temperate than Palmer. He marooned Palmer's golf cart in the mud—while Palmer was in it.

McGarrity was doing maintenance at the club tennis court when he was summoned by Palmer to drive him to his brother's house nearby. He doesn't remember the purpose. He doesn't remember the result. All he remembers is that Palmer was looking snazzy. "He was wearing these pastel pants and nice shoes," he said. "It was raining hard that day."

McGarrity needed to cross the road and inadvertently pulled the cart into the grass.

One press of the cart's accelerator and they were stuck. "So he gets out and takes a look," he said. "He's stomping around in the mud, not for a second worried about those shoes and those pastel pants."

Palmer's day was complicated by a necessary change of clothes, but if he was displeased with McGarrity, he kept it well concealed. "He acted like he wasn't mad at all," McGarrity said.

Lou Malik was 15 years old in 1969 and was following in the footsteps of his brothers by working as a locker room attendant at the club. The summer day was winding down, the guests had gone home, and he was gathering towels from the shower room when, lo and behold, his eyes caught a glint of treasure. There among the damp towels was a bejeweled timepiece.

"It was just sitting there on the corner," he said. "The thing must have weighed two pounds. It was a Rolex."

Care to take a wild guess as to whom it belonged? But the kid didn't turn it in, didn't even tell a soul about it. He, instead, tucked it away in a drawer in the shoeshine room. A night passed, and there were no inquiries. Nothing the first day either. Then on the second day, he was in the shoeshine room with his back to the door when he heard a familiar voice say, "Louie?"

He turned and said, "What can I do for you, Mr. Palmer?"

He asked if he'd seen a watch. "I told him, I had. I said it was big and heavy and was a Rolex. He said, 'Yeah, that's probably mine.'"

Then the kid asked Palmer to describe it. Palmer grinned, cocked his head, and asked Malik why he hadn't turned it in. "I said, 'Mr. Palmer, I knew whoever lost a watch that nice would come looking for it.'" And Malik thought he could safeguard it better than anyone else. Palmer seemed to like that answer, pulled out his wallet, and gave him a round number bill, either a $20 or a $50.

It's not the only time Malik had some of Palmer's gear. He not only cleaned Palmer's shoes, but he'd also sometimes borrow them. He wanted to see if he played any better in them than in his own, as if the secret was in the shoes. It was kind of like Mars Blackmon and the old Michael Jordan "It's gotta be the shoes" Nike commercials. Did he play like Palmer while wearing them? "Heck, no," he said. "But I'll say this: working at Latrobe Country Club for Arnold Palmer was the best job I ever had, loved every minute of it."

Chapter 6

The Golf Channel

A big-shot colleague of Izzy DeHerrera's was making some disparaging remarks from the passenger seat while rolling through a small town he was seeing for the first time. "He said, 'Hell, there's not a lot here is there?'" DeHerrera said. "And if you look at it just on the surface, he was right. Latrobe is one of those small towns that doesn't look special, but looks can be deceiving because Latrobe is definitely special. It'll always be a very special place to me. I was there 11 days and really fell in love with the place and the people."

DeHerrera, a Golf Channel producer, is one of those well-traveled sophisticates whose resume is studded with gaudy accomplishments from glamour spots around the globe. He's a 13-time Emmy Award winner and former NBC Sports feature producer who was pivotal to network coverage at multiple Super Bowls and Olympic games in Sydney, Turin, and Athens, to mention just a few. What the resume does not reflect is he's also a man of discerning insights about people and the places they all call home. "There's no place I've been that has as many down-to-earth people like there are in Latrobe," he said. "The people there have a joy and authenticity. You see it most clearly in Arnold

Palmer, but there's a spark of it in everyone you meet."

Based in Orlando, Florida, DeHerrera produced the much-lauded *Arnie*, the three-part life documentary for the Golf Channel that involved a crash-course immersion in Latrobe, Pennsylvania, Palmer, and what he calls "the power of home." He said getting the story of Palmer just right was the most important work he's ever done. "People all around the world were eager to know all they could about why this beloved icon, who could live anywhere, stayed at home in Latrobe," DeHerrera said.

He said home—no matter where home is—is a place or perhaps a fabled state of mind that bestows to each individual feelings of comfort, safety, and acceptance. It's something most everyone feels to a degree. Some ignore it and make peace with a certain drift. Others nurture it. "Arnold Palmer raised the power of home to something like a work of art," DeHerrera said. "I've never seen anything like it."

The sentiment hit him when he and his crew were filming Palmer on the scenic back tee at No. 10 at Latrobe Country Club. The tee box to the 203-yard par-3 is above a precarious outcrop of native shale. Falling from it would result in multiple traumas. "He was standing right on the edge of this cliff, and this is an 84-year-old man, and it's Arnold Palmer," he said. "I say, 'Excuse me, Mr. Palmer, but I'll feel better if you take a few steps away from the edge.' He got this real exasperated look and says, 'Young man! I've been standing right here on this edge my whole life. I'll be fine!'"

DeHerrera said he felt Latrobe's power of home in places like The Pond. He and his crew set up in The Pond's bar to do interviews with locals about their Palmer stories. "If you want to get a real sense of any town, you don't go to the T.G.I. Fridays on the highway," he said. "You find a really good local bar like The Pond and you just hang out there."

The results proved him correct. Narrated by Tom Selleck but

dominated by the homespun tales of unheralded storytellers, the critically-acclaimed program was a crossover sensation that became Golf Channel's most-watched and highest-rated original production ever.

The numbers and accolades pleased DeHerrera but nothing like the review he earned from one interested critic. Palmer had expressed some initial impatience with the grueling 11-day interview process. But the producer's enlightened thoroughness began to impress and engage the subject. "By the fourth day, he was really into it," he said, "and he'd answered the very last question."

The last question—and it's a good one—was: "Mr. Palmer, how fast did it all go by?"

He responded: "Oh, you can't believe how fast it all goes." Palmer appeared awestruck at the sum of his life and the realization it, like the interview, was concluding. DeHerrera took a deep breath and said, "That's it. We're done."

DeHerrera described the rest: "He gave me this big smile, pointed right at me, and said, 'You know, kid? You're pretty good!' That made me feel pretty special...Finding out that what everyone said about your hero was all true. He was as kind, as generous, and as wonderful as everyone had said he was."

To this day, when DeHerrera is feeling challenged by life's unsteady circumstances, he'll drive to Bay Hill, Florida, and seek solace communing with Palmer's spirit at the foot of his statue. What does he hear the statue say? "'C'mon! Suck it up! You can do this!'" DeHerrera said. "I can hear him telling me to give it my best, and it'll all work out."

The documentary was a huge personal and professional triumph for DeHerrera. It made a huge impact on the golf community. Golf Channel ran it multiple times during the week of Palmer's passing and memorial service, a week which brought a poignant mix of sadness and euphoria for men like DeHerrera.

On the way home from the service, DeHerrera and his companions decided a round of golf was the best way to shake off the blues. The men were still down and feeling bad about it, knowing Palmer wouldn't have abided the emotions. It's why they think his spirit had a hand in what happened next. DeHerrera got a hole in one, his first in 30 years of trying. "I pulled that ball out of the cup," he said, "looked up, smiled, and said, 'Thank you! I know you had something to do with this.'"

Chapter 7

Golfing Around the World

My honest exasperation with Arnold Palmer and his predictable golf routine led in 2012 to what I think was an answer that most revealed his true essence: when it comes to playing golf, Palmer is downright lazy.

I separate most golfers not by handicaps but in terms that relate to matrimony. They're either monogamists or polygamists. They're either satisfied playing the same steadfast course again and again or they like to play around—or a round—on different courses, enjoy different sights, and be confronted by new hazards and challenges.

What's bad for marriage can be good for golf. Sure, I enjoy rowdy rounds with my buddies on convenient locals, but if I had the means—if I was Palmer—I'd be daily jet-setting around the world to experience new and exotic courses.

Palmer was the exact opposite. He'd play Latrobe, Pennsylvania. Every day. All the time. He'd play Latrobe so routinely—what for many golfers would represent the checking off of a bucket list item by seeing Palmer playing golf at Latrobe—that it actually became a bit of a bore for the locals. *Well, there's Arnold Palmer teeing off on No. 2 at Latrobe again. Big whoop.*

It started getting to me, so one day I asked him about it. I said: "You're a founder of Laurel Valley, one of America's top 100 courses. It's just 15 minutes down the road. Yet you play it just four or five times a year. And you're a member at Oakmont, one of the top 10 courses in the world. It's an hour from your front door, but you play it maybe once a year. And if you wanted, you could just get in your jet and fly to Augusta, play, and be back home for dinner. Yet nearly every single day, you play Latrobe over and over, again and again. With all due respect, sir, what's wrong with you?"

He'd thoughtfully registered my sensible badgering and carefully weighed my arguments before giving his answer that was both simple and profound. "It's just so close," he said.

I think it's revelatory because it shows the man most associated with golf cared not at all about prestige or credentials. He cared only about playing golf. Don't mistake any of this as a knock on Latrobe Country Club, a challenging course I adore. You don't, of course, need to hear any endorsement from someone like me on Latrobe's appeal. But a man, who by some estimates played more golf than any man in history, played Latrobe more than any course and more than three times as much as Bay Hill, his second most-played course.

Palmer truly loved everything about Latrobe. He loved the layout, the facilities, the staff, the members, the conditions, the memories, the challenge, and that the first tee was just 1,987 feet from his front door. But his answer to me revealed that Palmer so loved playing golf that if he could have found a course that was just 1,986 feet from his front door then it would have become his go-to. He loved playing golf, but he cared more about the game than the prestige. To be fair, it's how he was with people, too.

That said, being the golfing great, Palmer, of course, did play golf all over the world—from Australia to China—at some of the best and most interesting courses that exist on this planet. In 2013 I asked Palmer if he had one week to travel the world and play all his favorite courses where would he go. He said: "Troon is one of my favorite golf courses. Birkdale. I like St. Andrews for a change from time to time. Wentworth is a course I enjoy. Domestically, there's Augusta, Oakmont, Winged Foot, all of the greats. On the Pacific I'm going to try and play Cypress Point when I'm out there next week. Not so much in the Far East. I won the Australian Open at the Royal Queensland Golf Club in Brisbane on the Gold Coast. That was very nice. I'd love to go back there." Here are the courses around the world Palmer has played.

Royal Queensland, Brisbane, Australia
(9,345 miles away from Latrobe, Pennsylvania)

He won the Australian Open there in 1966. Upon Palmer's passing, reporter Jim Tucker of *The Brisbane Courier-Mail* said Australia would forever be basking in his stardust. "Many of the thousands of fans assembled had never seen a helicopter much less a world star like Palmer," Tucker wrote. "He charmed, as always, with a set of borrowed clubs. Young fans frequently found the best vantage points in trees to ogle at the figure from black-and-white photos come to life in bold, blazing colour. Palmer wasn't afraid of a bit of climbing himself. Famously, he climbed a gum tree short of the 9th green at Victoria Golf Club in the 1964 Wills Masters to play his third shot some 5m off the ground."

Tucker wrote how former Australian Open champion Rodger Davis got an up-close idea of Palmer's hold on golf. "I played with him at

Metropolitan in Melbourne in a big event one year. I hit a shot and walked forward to pick up the divot and got bowled over to my knees by the gallery because in those days the fairways weren't roped off," Davis recalled. "I got to my feet, and Arnold said: 'Rodger, you don't replace divots when you are playing with me.' Keep up, in other words, because the gallery was there to see him."

Chung Shan Hot Springs Golf Course, Zhongshan City, China (8,013 miles away)

One of the first official acts decreed by Mao Zedong upon taking power in Communist China in 1949 was to ban golf because the game was an evident example of bourgeois excess.

It was nine years before a working class kid from a small factory town in Pennsylvania won his first major. And in 1982 hardline communists thought golf and Palmer were just what China's future needed. They thought golf would attract business. They hired Palmer and his course design team to make it happen.

Palmer recalled that the idea of golf was so alien to the local men who'd been hired to build the course that one of them tried to eat a golf ball. Palmer had to explain through an interpreter that it was a ball you hit. Today there are 500 golf courses in China, and Arnold Palmer Design Company has projects in 23 nations around the globe and in 38 different states.

Eiffel Tower, Paris, France (3,866 miles away)

In a promotional stunt on October 14, 1976, Palmer became the first person in the structure's then 87-year-old history to drive a golf ball from the 377-foot high second floor of the Eiffel Tower.

Arnold Palmer readies to drive a golf ball from the second floor of the Eiffel Tower in 1976. The balls landed in the Champs de Mars. *(AP Images)*

Club Campestre de Cali, Cali, Colombia (2,552 miles away)

Many Palmer fans are aware he had to leave the United States to win his first professional title. It was the 1955 Canadian Open. What fewer know is his second and third victories were outside the U.S. as well. In 1956 Palmer and a handful of other notables, including Roberto De Vicenzo, Bob Toski, and the then 43-year-old Sam Snead played in Colombia. He came from 7 strokes back in the final round to win by 2 strokes.

The previous week he and Snead outlasted the Panama Open field. The duo went head-to-head, and Palmer won a 6-hole sudden death playoff. The Panama victory earned the 26-year-old globetrotter a first-place check of $2,000.

Bandon Dunes, Bandon, Oregon (2,742 miles away)

The coast-clinging complex of courses in Oregon is widely renown among golfers as maybe the finest golf destination in America. It was renown by Palmer for another reason: he had to pay to play there. I learned this in June '15 when I was wondering if Palmer, a man who'd golfed as much as any who'd ever golfed, ever had to shell out green fees. It seemed likely that Palmer had rarely, if ever, been charged to play.

Think about it: his father was the local greenskeeper/club pro, so his childhood golf was free. Then he had high school and college years where he likely had team privileges so that was free. He may have been dinged for some greens fees during his years in the Coast Guard and selling paint in Cleveland. But by 1954 he'd become a pro golfer, and top courses around the world were paying him to play their tracks. His paying days were, it seemed, over.

Then he went to Bandon Dunes. "I've never really paid for playing golf anywhere except one time I went to golf with some friends at Bandon Dunes," Palmer said. "I can't forget the guy there saying, 'That will be $100, Mr. Palmer.' I guess that became sort of a slogan there. But I paid $100! The course was very interesting and very tough, but I won't be going back."

And he never did.

Pebble Beach Golf Links, Carmel-by-the-Sea, California (2,713 miles away)

My assignment in October 2015 was to interview Palmer about his love of cowboy films. I asked if he'd ever met John Wayne. "Never did," he said. "But I'm good friends with Clint Eastwood. We own Pebble Beach together, you know."

The pair were part of a group that in 1999 paid $820 million for the earthly Eden. He was very casual about saying he owned Pebble Beach, one of the world's most famous courses, like the way you'd tell someone about some DVD collection you possess.

I asked him how Clint was doing. He kind of shrugged in a sympathetic way and said, "Oh, he's okay. We're both 86 and we're both having the same kind of issues."

He said it in a way that conveyed growing old ain't for sissies. His tone led me to an impulsive question that immediately resurrected the steely competitor in the aging warrior: "Who'd win a wrestling match between you and Clint?"

"Oh, I'd kick his ass!"

It was hilarious. I think his reflexive outburst to challenge surprised him as being somehow impolite, and he tried to back down lest he offend Dirty Harry. "He has stand-ins," Palmer said. "I do all my own stunts."

Palmer owning Pebble Beach must have felt like pale reward after nearly 40 years of Pebble owning Palmer. His failures at Pebble were so striking that Neal Hotelling, author of the course's official history, *Pebble Beach Golf Links*, devoted several pages to the Pebble blot on Palmer's record in a chapter he calls, "The Greatest Golfer That Never Won." "In over 20 appearances, including an unbroken run from 1958 through 1971, Palmer failed to record a win at Pebble Beach," Hotelling said. "During that same period, he had four wins at The Masters, one U.S. Open, and two wins at the British Open. It's not that Palmer had no luck at Pebble Beach, but rather that the luck he had was all bad."

True, a less gracious man than Palmer might have purchased Pebble Beach and out of vengeance turned the pristine property into a cow pasture, thus denying the public of ever seeing what all agree is some of the most scenic territory in the world. One group that was never disappointed with Palmer's often ill-fated exploits at Pebble Beach were sportswriters. A generation of great sports scribes honed their skills on Palmer adventures at Pebble.

In 1964 Palmer hit long on the 17th hole. Rather than risk disqualification, he found and played the ball, opting for a risky shot instead of taking a 1-stroke penalty for an unplayable lie. As golfer and commentator Jimmy Demaret explained it to the television audience, Palmer had the option of dropping along a line behind the original position of the ball. "In that case," Demaret said, "his nearest drop would be Honolulu."

So Palmer gamely played the ball and was joined on the rocks as a wandering dog stood with head cocked nearby. Famed sportswriter Jim Murray of the *Los Angeles Times* was watching from home on his television and later wrote: "Palmer was so far out on the moor in the ocean he looked like Robinson Crusoe. His only companions were a dog and a sand wedge. I thought for a minute or so we had switched channels and Walt Disney was bringing us a heartwarming story of a boy and his dog, but a companion, peering closer had a better idea. 'Shouldn't that dog have a cask around his neck?'"

Bay Hill Club & Lodge, Orlando, Florida (969 miles away)

One is beloved for making people happy and shaping decades of lucrative tourism for The Sunshine State. The other is Mickey Mouse. That's what Pat Williams, then-president of the NBA's Orlando Magic, told the *Orlando Sentinel* in 2006. He said Palmer is one of two people most responsible for the explosive growth of the central Florida boom. "He had the vision way ahead of anybody else," Williams said. "If I had to pick two people who had the biggest impact on what Orlando has become, I'd pick Arnold Palmer and Walt Disney."

And Orlando had a mighty big impact on Palmer. If he loved Latrobe—and he clearly did—he doted on Orlando in general and Bay Hill in particular. He built and maintained renown hospitals, led worthy charity drives, and hosted a signature PGA event there.

He fell in love with the then modest property in 1965 when he was a 33-year-old sensation and looking for a place to keep his game sharp through the winters. "Back then, it was really quiet and sort of out-of-the way," he said. "And it had a nice golf course. I decided it would make the perfect winter home."

He took ownership of Bay Hill in '75 and was ceaseless in his tinkering of both the club and the course. "I just love everything about it," he said in 2015. "Latrobe will always be home, but Bay Hill is special to me. But I've traveled so much that I really enjoy just being home in Latrobe and home in Orlando at Bay Hill. I really am looking forward to spending whatever time I have left in those two places."

A competent psychoanalyst would no doubt be exhilarated by the opportunity to put both Latrobe and Bay Hill on the couch to examine what amounts to a sibling rivalry over Palmer's affections. It's mostly subtle, but spend enough time talking to familiars, and it becomes clear Latrobe partisans are attuned to any perceived slight initiated by their Southern overseers.

It made the local papers when shortly after the boss' death, most of his long-time office staff were encouraged to abruptly and all at once retire. It made business sense, certainly. Why maintain a Palmer satellite office when Palmer won't be coming back? For years now many of the top decision makers in Arnold Palmer Enterprises have resided year-round in Orlando.

The sole exception being, ahem, Mr. Palmer himself.

Particularly irksome to locals was the Orlando-directed order that distribution of popular umbrella lapel pins has become regulated. The size of umbrella-shaped Tic Tacs, there must be a million of these pleasing little freebies in circulation. But ever since Palmer's death, everyone who requests one either in person or by mail must submit to Bay Hill their name and address before being deemed worthy. So the tiny trinkets that office staff in general and Palmer in particular used to hand out like Halloween candy are now subject to petty bureaucracy. And what was once joyful and pure is yet again sacrificed to the altar of craven marketing.

Personally, I've never understood any conflict. I love visiting Bay Hill and have been treated with what seemed to me to be flattering attention when my hosts learned I lived in Latrobe. In fact, Palmer fostered amiable connections by graciously setting up countless Latrobe club members with Bay Hill privileges. He'd often do the same for non-members.

But the grumbles persist. As news of Palmer's death was spreading, it wasn't uncommon to hear neighbors express a tasteless relief that, gee, if he had to die, at least he did so close to home, as if Orlando was behind enemy lines. Maybe it's the small town psyche, a need to prove to cosmopolitan cynics that small town doesn't mean default rube. Or—and this is bound to sound unfairly parochial—but maybe our Bay Hill friends suffer from an inferiority complex.

They understand it took Latrobe to make Arnold Palmer, and it took Arnold Palmer to make Bay Hill.

Harbour Town Golf Links, Hilton Head, South Carolina (685 miles away)

This one might seem an odd inclusion. After all, Harbour Town was built in 1967 by Pete Dye and Jack Nicklaus. That no one will dispute. But many historians will contend it was Palmer who truly made Harbour Town and Hilton Head.

The old veteran hadn't won in 14 months, and many said his best days were far behind him. The flashy tournament rookie course needed to make a good impression or risk being relegated to second-tier status in a PGA field crowded with other worthy aspirants. Promoters say Palmer's surprise 1969 victory at the first Heritage Classic literally put the island on the map. "Palmer saved us," recalled John Gettys Smith in 1994. Smith was a public relations executive for Sea Pines Resort, the island tip development that became the model for hundreds of other coastal Southern gated communities eager to capitalize on northerners' love for sunshine and golf. "His win brought us instant recognition."

Harbour Town was the first golf course design that Nicklaus—under the tutelage of Pete Dye—ever worked on. With its landmark lighthouse as the backdrop for the 18th green along Calibogue Sound, it remains one of the top golf courses in the country. But as with many fledgling tournaments, it was having trouble attracting attention for the tournament then held during the busy Thanksgiving weekend.

A last-minute withdrawal left promoters scrambling to fill a high-profile spot. They called Palmer. He agreed to play but only on the condition that he could land his plane at the still-under-construction airport. It was arranged, and photographers snapped pictures of Palmer carrying his golf bag from his plane.

Columnist Jim Littlejohn, who wrote for a Hilton Head newspaper, recalled in 1991 how veteran golf writer Charles Price told naysayers that Palmer's mere participation would assure success. Littlejohn wrote, "Everyone kept asking Price who'd be playing, and he'd always say, 'Nicklaus will play in it because he helped design it, and with Nicklaus and Palmer, you won't need anyone else.'"

Palmer did more than play. Coming off a four-week tour layoff, he vowed to put persistent putting woes "out of my mind or die trying." In addition, he'd been doing 50 sit-ups each evening and again in the morning to strengthen his ailing hip. A 1-under-par 70 gave him a 3-stroke lead going into the final day and brought with it a flood of national reporters to the remote island to write another series of euphoric "Palmer's back!" stories.

He wound up fending off Dick Crawford and Bert Yancey and did a mock stagger across the 18th green into the arms of Nicklaus before being given the $20,000 first-place check. Pictures from the victory show a grinning Palmer holding the trophy with the skeleton of what was the still-unfinished landmark lighthouse in the background. "Our little press tent was barely able to handle the huge surge of reporters from all over the country," Smith said. "But by Monday there were stories all around the world about Palmer's big win at Harbour Town. It's impossible to calculate what the Palmer win meant for Hilton Head."

It was easier for affable Latrobe attorney Chuck Mason, who in 1990 was representing Palmer in a suit filed in a Hilton Head court. A Latrobe Country Club member, Mason believes in being prepared for any eventuality. That means in addition to all his legal briefs, Mason brought his golf bag, the one that had a prominent Latrobe bag tag attached at the strap. Today, it costs as much as $250 to play 18 at Harbour Town. Mason doesn't know how much it cost in '90, but his round was free. "I was at the bag drop, and one of the starters saw my Latrobe bag tag and says, 'Are you here on behalf of Mr. Palmer?' I told him I was. And he said, 'Then your round is on the house.' They still had a real reverence for what Arnold had done for them just by showing up all those years ago."

Mason won his Palmer case as well. Did the presiding judge happen to be a Palmer fan, too? "I always win my cases based on my astute presentation of the facts," he said. "But it never hurt when the judge was a golfer who loved Arnold Palmer."

Chapter 8

Local Golf Courses

Arnold Palmer played all over the world, of course, but he loved playing at Latrobe Country Club. Here are some other favorite courses that were relatively close in proximity to his Pennsylvania home.

The Palmer Course at Stonewall Resort, Roanoke, West Virginia (131 miles away from Latrobe, Pennsylvania)

Sometimes the roles would be reversed, and Arnold Palmer would ask me the questions: "How's your family?" "Staying busy?" And—always—"have you been golfing?"

In October of 2011, I told him my family was fine, I could stand to be a little busier, and the week before I'd played a round at one of my all-time favorite courses. That got his attention. He wanted to know where. I told him the course is in Roanoke, West Virginia. "That's my course! Everyone loves Stonewall," he said. The Palmer team designed it, and Palmer played it after hitting the ceremonial first tee shot May 30, 2002.

I already knew all that. I just liked hearing my opinion ratified by the world's most famous golfer. Palmer's always been reluctant to appear to show favoritism of one of his designed courses over another, but there's always been something special about Stonewall. For me, it'll always be special for sentimental reasons. I wrote some of the first national reviews of it when it opened in 2002. And it was the last course my father ever set foot on before he died in 2004.

I've gone back at least once a year often with Palmer's brother, Jerry, or his personal assistant, Doc Giffin. And for years the Latrobe pro shop staff and friends would make the two-hour drive south down I-79 to spend the day at Stonewall. They, too, love the course. To anyone familiar with the Latrobe clubhouse, Stonewall feels right at home. It's pure Palmer. "We'll always be incredibly proud of our association with Arnold Palmer," said director of golf Randy Hernly. "We do everything we can to highlight and honor that relationship. It's very special to everyone at Stonewall."

The walls of the pro shop and second floor dining room, Lightburn's Restaurant, are packed with Palmer photos, letters, and laudatory magazine articles. At the base of the staircase is a 10-foot oaken Arnie statue carved from hardwood. The lavish Palmer documentary runs on a continuous loop in every guest room on the dedicated lodge channel. The Palmer reverence extends to Jerry, who Hernly called "one of the nicest guys in the world."

Arnold Palmer seemed to take real pleasure that so many of his Latrobe neighbors reveled in the scenic West Virginia course. I asked him in 2014 about it, and he confessed to some paternal pride. "Oh, I'm very pleased with how things have turned out at Stonewall," he said. "It was such a magnificent piece of wilderness, and we're proud of that fine course. They've done a great job of promoting it with a fine hotel and the golf course and all they have to offer. All my friends, who know it, tell me they really love Stonewall. They enjoy going there to play and say it's the perfect venue for golf, very picturesque. I wish Randy and all the people down there all the best of luck."

Gary Player had been in the running for course architect, but the consensus always came back to Palmer. "He meant so much to golf and to the world, and the caliber of the people who represent him have always been the best," Hernly said. "We've found that if someone knows or knew Arnold Palmer they would always try and embody the best of Arnold Palmer. And that's a tradition we try and carry on here at Stonewall. And that's never going to change."

The Old Course at Bedford Springs, Bedford Springs, Pennsylvania (58 miles away)

This beguiling valley course is notable not just for its innate beauty, but also because it is as far (or near, really) as I can tell to the closest destination Palmer ever flew his jet to play golf.

This was the man who in 1976 set an aviation record by flying a Learjet 36 around the world in 57 hours, 25 minutes, and 42 seconds. With capability of reaching 700 mph, it only took 12 minutes to fly to the Bedford County Airport. Passenger and playing partner Dr. Jimmy Bryan said, "[It] took us twice that to commute from the airport to the course."

Oakmont Country Club, Oakmont, Pennsylvania (37 miles away)

Palmer told me in 2006 that as a mere boy he used to dream of winning tournaments at fabled Oakmont Country Club, just an hour west of Latrobe. The dream came true at a very early age. "I was just a kid when I beat Jack Benson there to win the 1949 Western Pennsylvania Amateur," he recalled. "Oakmont is so full of tradition from the locker room to men standing and laughing in the wooden floored barroom. The course is always in excellent condition. It just really resonates with all

Arnold Palmer's putt on the 18th green rolls just past the cup, forcing him into a playoff with Jack Nicklaus during the epic 1962 U.S. Open at Oakmont Country Club. (AP Images)

that's great about golf. At 18, it was such an unbelievable thrill to win there."

That win, however, is a mere asterisk in Palmer's career at the course that's brought more misery than majesty. It was at Oakmont where the symbolic changing of the guard took place in 1962 when Jack Nicklaus beat Palmer and an often belligerent crowd of Palmer stalwarts to win the U.S. Open. And in 1973 Palmer stood on the 12th green as the final round leader of that year's U.S. Open when he was stunned to see Johnny Miller had posted a record-setting 63 to vault to victory. And it was at Oakmont in 1994 that Palmer closed the door on his U.S. Open career before a crowd so adoring that tears spilled down the old golfer's face as their 18th green ovation washed over him.

In fact, tears are Oakmont's only water hazard. It is a heartbreaker. Forty-four years after the watershed tournament, Palmer still sounded mournful when talking about the '62 Open and how he let it get away. "I used to putt those greens pretty well when I was younger, but in '62 Nicklaus beat me on the greens by 17 shots...17!" He'd said, sounding as if he could snap a stout-shafted putter over his knee at the bitter recollection.

Bob Ford was Oakmont's head pro from 1980 to 2017 and had golfed there with Palmer many times. Not once, he said, had forward-focused Palmer stepped out of character and gazed backward. Not once did he stop to dwell on the past—until 2006. Ford said Palmer had stopped by on July 11, 2006, to play a round prior to the Major League Baseball All-Star festivities occurring that day at Pittsburgh's PNC Park. "That's the only time I've ever played with him that he even got the slightest bit reflective," Ford said. "Never once did he look back or mention past tournaments until that recent summer day."

Ford said Palmer stood at the side of 9th green of the par-5 hole and recalled how he'd been at that spot in 1962 in two shots. He told Ford how he'd been just off the green, right next to the flag with idealistic thoughts of birdie, maybe even a pivotal eagle. But a chagrined Palmer recalled how he flubbed a clip and how the greens took a bite out of his ambitions and he stalked off with a discouraging bogie. "Then on 12th green, he said how he stood there in 1973 and had been head-to-head in the lead with Julius Boros when both looked up at the leader board and saw Johnny Miller had posted his record-setting 63 on the rain-damped greens," Ford said. "He couldn't believe it."

As the round continued, Ford said he was struck by how nostalgic Palmer was going through the years and rounds that are indelibly etched into the history of one of America's most legendary courses. "I got the feeling that maybe he thought it was one of the last times he'd ever play there," Ford said. "And it saddened me to think Arnold Palmer was having those thoughts."

But in the end, it won't be those wistful moments Ford said he'll recall from an otherwise ordinary round with an extraordinary gentleman. It won't be Palmer talking about tournaments and titles that got away four decades ago. It won't be the echoes of the cheers and the reciprocal love between a hometown boy who'd gone global and the fans who loved him so fiercely for both his successes and failures. No, Ford said the recollection he'll most cherish happened before the round even started. And the unlikely instigators were some scrawny youths clinging to a fence separating the Oakmont pool from the nearby first tee. "We were getting ready to tee off and we heard these kids applauding," Ford said. "We turned around and a bunch of the boys had climbed out of the water and were hanging on the fence to watch Arnold Palmer tee off. They hadn't even been born when he won his last tournament, but they were cheering him like he was Tiger Woods. He smiled, waved, turned to me, and said, 'Bob, that's what keeps bringing me out after all these years.' It made me tingle all over. That's what I'll always remember most about that day. That's the memory I'll cherish."

Champion Lakes Golf Club, Bolivar, Pennsylvania (16 miles away)

He's a world-renown athlete of unparalleled achievement. He owns one of the best courses in western Pennsylvania, and gushing strangers still stop him to chat about the glory days. But I'm not talking about Palmer.

No, I'm talking about Dick Groat, who was a famous two-sport athlete before Deion Sanders ever got his ear pierced. He was a five-time Major League Baseball All-Star, the 1960 MVP, and won a World Series championship as the Pittsburgh Pirates' shortstop during the 1960 season when Bill Mazeroski hit one of the most famous home runs in baseball history. He was a two-time All-American guard for the Duke University Blue Devils and was the first player in that hallowed program's history to have his number (10) retired. He played for the NBA's now-defunct Fort Wayne Pistons, and his smiling face has three times graced the cover of *Sports Illustrated*.

And with former Pirates player Jerry Lynch, Groat designed and built Champion Lakes Golf Club in 1966 near Ligonier, Pennsylvania, about 20 minutes down the road from Latrobe Country Club. With its lush, whisker-wide fairways, the course has for four decades been one of the most challenging and best conditioned in Pennsylvania and has been named by *Golf Digest* as among the top 50 public courses in America.

You'd think an athlete as accomplished as Groat would feel a kinship with a fellow superstar with substantial roots in the golf industry. Think again. "I've never once felt like a peer around Arnold Palmer," said Groat, who turned 87 in 2017. "I was a pretty good ballplayer and could play some basketball, but Arnold was the very best at his sport. He was the undisputed top gun in golf, always will be."

Groat's fondness for Palmer stems also, he admitted, from what Palmer meant to Groat's post-athletic career. "Nobody ever says baseball players were smart, and I proved that when I built a golf course right in Arnold Palmer's backyard," he said. "But he and his brother Jerry were nothing but enormous pluses for us our entire 51 years. They're always referring players from Latrobe Country Club to come out and give us a try."

More than even that personal connection is what Palmer did for golf in general. "There's never been anyone who, and I mean anyone, who did for a sport what Arnold Palmer did for golf," Groat said. "People followed him to the golf course like he was the Pied Piper. There've been great players since who people enjoy watching on TV, but Arnold's been the only one who made people want to pick up a club and go out and play golf. And he's done it all with warmth and class."

Groat was with Palmer step-for-step in 1968 when the Latrobe pro shot the course-record 68 at the par-71 Champion Lakes, a record that stood for more than 20 years until local upstart Rocco Mediate shaved 2 strokes off Palmer's mark. "You should have seen it," Groat said. "Palmer was joking the whole time and, man, some of the shots he hit. Boy, could he play. That day with Arnie is something I'll never forget."

It said something about Palmer that Groat, a man who's been on the field for some of the most remarkable moments in sports history, remembers a friendly, noncompetitive round with a fellow golf course owner with the same enthusiasm and clarity that he remembers things like Mazeroski's monumental home run.

Laurel Valley Golf Club, Ligonier, Pennsylvania (10 miles away)

Built in 1959 Laurel Valley was audaciously conceived to be nothing less than Augusta North. Today, Laurel has beauty, immaculate conditioning, enormous prestige, stately facilities for the well-heeled, and some history even Augusta can't touch. After all, it hosted the 1975 Ryder Cup. And Laurel had Palmer.

So is Augusta likely to become Laurel South? No chance of that. Augusta is Augusta. And Doc Giffin and I one day surmised that Palmer played Augusta more times than any courses besides Latrobe and Bay Hill. He played The Masters from 1955 to 1983 without missing a cut. That's 112 rounds—not counting recreational rounds with guys like Ike. Then he played the next 21 rounds before bowing out in 2004. (That's a minimum of 84 rounds, but let's graciously round up to 100.) That's 212 rounds during Masters week alone.

So Palmer played Augusta, but Palmer built Laurel. He told me so in 2006. "I've been with Laurel since the very beginning," said Palmer, who was involved in multiple touch-ups. "There were nine guys at the original planning meeting, and I was one of them. I was the one who advised them to select architect Dick Wilson to design the course. I had a great relationship with the founders. I was pleased when they asked me to be the touring pro for Laurel Valley, and it's a position I held throughout my playing career. It's always been a very special place to me and it always will be."

The feeling is mutual. Cloyd Goddard, a retired school teacher, has been at Laurel since 1987 when he began as a caddie. He recalled the time he was raking a bunker on the 2nd hole when he casually asked Palmer if he needed any help reading the snaky 15-foot putt. Palmer's response: "Did you forget who built this green?"

"Then," Goddard said, "he sunk the putt."

Today Goddard is the greeter and the first person most guests see. When a few years back, word reached Palmer that Goddard was battling prostate cancer, Palmer reacted with concerned magnanimity. "He put his arm around me, pulled me close, and said, 'Now, Cloyd, if there's anything at all you need, don't be afraid to call. And I mean anything.' I knew he meant it, too," Goddard said.

Why wouldn't he? He loved Laurel and all its people. Here, Palmer made the flattering comparison. "I get much the same exhilarating feeling when I drive up to the clubhouse between the rows of stately pines at Laurel that I do when I head down Magnolia Lane at Augusta National and The Masters," Palmer said. "It means that much to me."

Glengarry Golf Links, Latrobe, Pennsylvania (5.3 miles away)

Jim Beattie, a Ligonier local, was on the 427-yard par-4, 17th hole at Glengarry Golf Links at 3:29 PM on September 29, 2016, when he saw something that made him stop thinking about the green. He was too captivated by the whole magnificent spectrum. It was a rainbow but not just any rainbow. It was Arnie's Rainbow.

Rainbows are naturally occurring meteorological phenomena. The bible says God used a rainbow to signify his covenant between Him and all Earth's living creatures. One can only speculate what Arnie's Rainbow meant. "It was the coolest thing," Beattie said. "It was four days after he'd died. We were almost finishing up at Glengarry when I see this plane flying right over Glengarry. I knew it was Arnie's plane."

What he did not know at the time was Palmer copilot Pete Luster had taken his friend's ashes for one last flight over Latrobe. A light cloudburst coincided with takeoff. The clouds parted, and soon area residents were looking up in wonder as the man many know as Pete the Pilot flew a jet that seemed to spark a vibrant rainbow. A picture snapped from the end of an airport runway seemed to show the rainbow linking Latrobe and the country club. The timing and the Palmer connection may have caused some Internet cynics to suspect deft photoshopping, a common outbreak of fake news. But it happened. We all saw it. "It's something I'll never forget," Beattie said. "And to see it right over a Latrobe golf course gave me chills."

It wasn't the first time Palmer bestowed this fun local course—a favorite of area golf leagues—with a splash of color. Glengarry's director of golf Jamie Costic remembered back in 2008 when Palmer and some friends showed up to play. "It was surreal," he said. "No one wanted to bother him about pictures, but he insisted. He was very complimentary about the course. We get a lot of local play, and I think he just wanted to see Glengarry for himself. Having Arnold Palmer just show up to play our course, man, that's something I'll never forget."

Costic says he still receives a lot of golfing out-of-towners eager to know if Palmer's ever played there and if he was as nice as everyone always says. "I tell them he's just like everyone says," Costic points out, "real down-to-earth."

Latrobe Elks Lodge Golf Club, Latrobe, Pennsylvania (5.6 miles away)

My buddies and I were golfing at the Elks one fall day in 2000 when we saw a snazzy black Escalade pull up right near the pro shop where they park the carts. The brashness of the move didn't go unnoticed by our group as we made our way between the 9th green and the 10th tee. We were all thinking, *Who does this guy think he is? Arnold Palmer?*

It turns out he thinks that exactly because it was Palmer, himself, who emerged from the vehicle. Enchanted isn't an emotion usually associated with paunchy middle-aged men, but I confess to feeling enchanted. We were seeing The Man in his native habitat. It wasn't Latrobe Country Club, a private club we couldn't play. It felt better than that. At some point during that morning, both Palmer and I shared the exact same thought: *Today would be a great day to play the Elks!*

And, indeed, it was.

In Latrobe a lot of golfers think that every day. The Elks is tough, fair, and it and its lightning greens are always in excellent shape. What I remember most about that day—and this was four years before I sensed he'd have a tangible role in my life—was when Palmer walked into the bar for post-round beers. Again, just like me and the regular ol' Joes. It was an instant Mardi Gras. Everyone's mood dramatically improved because everyone who wanted a Palmer autograph knew they were going to get one. And the rest of us were going to get a really good story. Pro Rick Battaglia said it had been like that at the Elks for years. "He played here a lot in the '50s and '60s and for years held the course record," he said. "It was a 62 or maybe a 63. And he was a social member for years. You would have never known he was rich and famous. He was just like a regular person."

An Act of Grace on the Home Course

You can, of course, hear myriad great Palmer stories at Latrobe Country Club. But you can no longer for just a few bucks purchase in the pro shop what to me is the greatest Palmer story ever told. More like never told. The pro shop used to sell souvenir Latrobe Country Club bag tags, which were about the size of a playing card. On the front was the LCC logo and "ARNIE'S BEST EVER." On the back was a re-creation of the scorecard and a hole-by-hole tally of what he shot on July 13, 1969. The back, by the way, also listed "M.J. (Deke) Palmer" as club professional. It was a keepsake of the best round he ever shot anywhere under any circumstances.

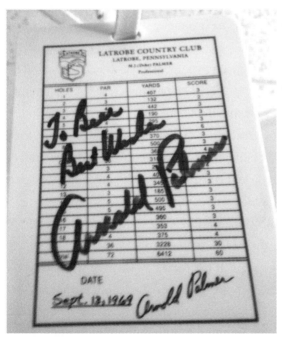

This golf bag tag commemorates Arnold Palmer's epic round on July 13, 1969. *(Chris Rodell)*

But the story of that great round goes beyond the numbers. It includes the hope, the triumph, the anger, the resolve, and the eventual acceptance of eternal frustration that dogged him five decades hence. "I still remember every shot like it was yesterday," he told me in 2007. "I had a lot of great shots that day, but I'm still haunted by some of the ones I missed."

Never played Latrobe? Let the maestro describe it. "Think about Latrobe Country Club as an older golf course that is very demanding on direction," Palmer said, "not so much on distance but one that will keep you thinking and your mind working to score well."

His mind was working very well that day. He'd set a club record that still stands, though it now stands because of the humble grace of his adoring friend Bob Ford, Oakmont's head pro from 1980 to 2017. A course record usually still involves one that got away. With Palmer that day, it was more like five. He was 4-under after 5 and "feeling pretty good," he said. "I had every reason to believe it was going to continue."

No. 6 is a 466-yard par-5. If you're Palmer on a tear you're thinking eagle. "The thought did cross my mind," he said.

How easy is No. 6? I've reached it in two. Palmer, inexplicably, took a bogie 6. It ticked him off enough for him to score a 3 on both 7 and 8, a par-4 and 5, respectively. He then parred No. 9, a gentle uphill dogleg right. His front 9 score was 30.

I always describe Latrobe's front nine as claustrophobic. Holes 5, 6, and especially 7, are like high school hallways with oaks, pines, and maples lined like lockers. But the back 9 immediately grants some outlook-adjusting breathing room. It settles the mind and allows for more aggression. If that's how Palmer felt, he was immediately humbled by the relatively benign 203-yard par-3 10th. He bogied. "I knew I had a chance to for the first time break 60," he said. "And to start off with a bogie on 10, well, that set me off."

He played as well as he ever had over the next six holes: birdie, birdie, par, eagle, eagle, birdie. He was minus-7 over six. So his back nine was at 22—52 for the round with two fair par-4s awaiting. A milestone 59— maybe even a remarkable 58—was within his grasp. He must have been salivating coming to the downhill 342-yard par-4 17th. Why wouldn't he? It's the 18th handicap hole, the easiest on the course. But he missed the birdie putt for a tap-in par.

He was at 56 on the way to the last hole. The 18th is a more worthy opponent at 377 yards. After the drive it's a steep uphill second shot to a sloped green. His second shot left him a snaky 15-footer. "I thought I had it," he said. "I really did, but it missed. I still really kick myself for that bogie on 6."

It has to be one of the most flawed course-record 60s in golf history. Turn the two bogeys into pars and one of the five pars into a birdie, and the Latrobe course record is 57. Get a little more creative, and 55 isn't out of the question, right? Not to Palmer. "With a round like that," he said, "so many shots can go one way or the other."

In the 1999 Palmer Cup, an annual Latrobe event that pits the area's best club professionals versus the best amateurs, Ford was feeling it, in a zone like no other. Palmer that day was in the group ahead of Ford and certainly must have seen some of Ford's stick-rattling magic. Led by a double eagle on the par-5 3rd hole, Ford was 9-under after 14, clearly on pace to either tie or surpass The King, and Palmer was watching.

What happened next is still discussed among soul-searching golfers familiar with the facts. And the question is asked: what would you do? Well, here's what Ford did. He picked up. He withdrew.

Ford's opponent that day, top amateur Sean Knapp, told golf writer Gerry Dulac of the *Pittsburgh Post-Gazette*, he wanted to see him continue: "I've played with many people on the PGA Tour, and it was as fine a round of golf as I've ever seen. There was no telling how low he was going to go."

Breaking Palmer's record, Ford said, never crossed his mind. "I'd never dream of doing that—not in front of The King." Instead he went up ahead and watched Palmer finish.

Chapter 9

Tom Ridge

Tom Ridge, a decorated Vietnam veteran, served as our nation's Director of Homeland Security during the tumultuous years following the devastating September 11, 2001 attacks. Prior to that patriotic duty, he was Pennsylvania's governor during scandal-free years of statewide prosperity. Lately, liberty-loving governments from around the globe seek his advice on a vast array of modern security issues. But get him talking today, and it sounds like he's gunning for another position: president of the Latrobe-area chamber of commerce. "To me, Latrobe is one of those great central Pennsylvania Norman Rockwell towns," he said. "It has so much to offer people from all over the world. I just love that town."

The state that Ridge presided over was rich in timber, oil, fertile soil, and natural beauty, but he said our greatest natural resource was stripped from us September 25, 2016. "The death of Arnold Palmer was a terrible loss," he said. "More than a year later and I still think of him every day. There's still so much he has to teach us about life, about humanity, and how to embrace and uplift one another the Arnold Palmer way."

And Latrobe, Pennsylvania, was Palmer's classroom. "That great man is so internationally iconic and so tied to his hometown roots," he said. "We need to find a way to build on his legacy, and Latrobe must be the epicenter."

He's been thinking about this for a year and he's been setting aside his sentiments and thinking about it in terms of infrastructure, funding, and marketing. He's been thinking about it the way a policy wonk would. Nearby airport? Check. Lodging? Check. Street access? Check. And those essentials are all named Arnold Palmer. Ridge believes in turning Latrobe into an iconic tourist destination and having federal, state, and local governments partner with private interests so that it's done right. "There's no question there's an enormous appetite to perpetuate his legacy," he said. "People are always going to want to see the town where he grew up, see his workshop, his office, his memorabilia, and play the course where he grew up."

And there is local precedent. St. Vincent College is home to the Fred Rogers Center for Early Learning and Children's Media. The $15 million center opened in 2006 and includes 16,000 Rogers-related items that are being mined for insights on how to best teach children.

Rogers was awarded his Presidential Medal of Freedom in 2002, two years before Palmer. When I pointed this out to him in '10, Palmer actually seemed ticked, as if it bothered him that gentle, beloved Fred Rogers earned the accolade before him. Now, *that's* a competitor.

And St. Vincent is already home to the Winnie Palmer Nature Reserve, a 50-acre wonderland incorporated in 2000 as both an environmental asset and natural bulwark against unsightly corporate sprawl. Could St. Vincent one day be home to an Arnold Palmer Athletic Pavilion and Legacy Museum? Ridge wouldn't rule it out. "All the assets that people want to see are right there in Latrobe," he said. "It just needs some constructive unification."

Former Director of Homeland Security Tom Ridge, who said Arnold Palmer would have made a terrific politician and public servant, caddies for Palmer. *(Howdy Giles)*

One item future archivists won't be getting their hands on is a picture of Ridge and Palmer, arms around one another, and laughing together on some sunny fairway. It's one of his most prized possessions. He remembers the time at Laurel Valley—it was fall, Ridge's favorite season to be outdoors in the Keystone State—and the friends were strolling toward their approach shots. "The foliage was peak color, and the blue sky had all these puffy clouds in that blue sky," he said. "He stopped, held out his arms, and said, 'Hey, Tom, look around. This is my office. Now do you understand why I love to go to work?'"

Ridge talks about his friend the way kids talk about Santa Claus. "He just had this warmth about him, where if he gave you that big thumbs-up, you felt like you'd been his best friend for life," he said. "And the great thing about Arnold was he was like that with Fortune 500 CEOs and the locker room attendant. I've never known another individual so embedded with so much humanity. I miss him every single day."

He much preferred Palmer as a friend to having him as a potential political opponent. "Had he run for either governor or president even," Ridge said, "he'd have made a damn fine candidate with a great chance of winning."

Ridge points out Palmer was imbued with all the qualities politicians either hone or contrive. He had name identification, tremendous success, and extreme likability. And, as noted, he was competitive. Any man who was ticked about being bested by Mister Rogers would make mincemeat out of your typical pol. And you'd think he'd enjoy the challenge of confounding any experts who said a golfer couldn't win.

The hypothetical reminds Ridge of a time when Palmer hit his ball about ankle deep in the water. It was behind the yellow stakes. Every other golfer would have declared an unplayable lie, taken a penalty stroke, dropped it, and moved on. It was, after all, just a friendly round. "Not him. No, he puts one foot in the water and soaks it," Ridge said. "Then he hits this spectacular shot out, splashing mud and water all over himself in the process. I looked at him and asked why he didn't take an unplayable lie. He said, 'Tom Ridge, did you just see me hit a good shot out of there?'"

Ridge said, indeed, he had. "Then it wasn't unplayable, now, was it?" Palmer said.

Chapter 10

Random Acts of Palmer

The good deeds happened with so much cheerful regularity that I asked John Rusbosin if they were maybe the work of fairies or elves. "More like angels," he said. This happened in communities around the country, of course, but it felt more pronounced in Latrobe, Pennsylvania, because the motivating force behind so many of the good deeds was Arnold Palmer. He understood his every gesture, especially in Latrobe, would be magnified, maybe emulated.

In the end the magnification reflected something beautiful. "It was a mind-set of doing good because doing good wasn't only helpful and proper, but because doing good also feels good," Rusbosin said. "It makes the world a better place. It's spiritual."

Rusbosin knew a thing or two about that. His numerous charitable activities make the world a better place, while his professional ones make it more comfortable. He owns Rusbosin Furniture, the store across U.S. Route 30 from the main runway at Arnold Palmer Regional Airport. Bob Rusbosin, a father of 11, opened the business in 1963, and today it is a Route 30 landmark that doubles as a visual cue to trigger safe landings.

It's the kind of local business where high school groups on summer weekends raise money for things like band uniforms by offering to scrub your car outside of Rusbosin's store for $5. And the store website proudly states how it stands for more than 100 local charities. Beneficiaries include St. Vincent College, Latrobe Area Hospital, and Christ the Divine Teacher School. The Arnold Palmer Spirit of Hope Award benefits Latrobe's Adelphoi Village, a center for disadvantaged youth. With Palmer's high-profile involvement, the charity has raised more than $3 million since 2005. When it comes to giving, what is the Palmer spirit? "I never knew him to say no to any request, especially ones involving helping local children. He'd often donate anonymously," Rusbosin said. "And he'd often ask the amount of the highest bid so he could match it."

As community service officer for the Pennsylvania State Police, trooper Steve Limani started from scratch the popular Shop With a Cop program to purchase Christmas gifts for underprivileged children or those traumatized by crime. He told Palmer he'd raised $40,000, a goal that assured crucial sustainability for years to come. "I told him all about it," he said. "He asked a lot of questions and sounded interested. So I was a little surprised when I didn't hear from him. I thought for sure I would."

He eventually heard from him alright—loud and clear. He was asked to visit Palmer's office and given an envelope, which he resisted opening until he was back in his patrol car. "It was a check for $50,000," Limani said.

He was crossing his fingers, hoping it would be $5,000. Limani asked later if Palmer wanted the donation publicized. He humbly did not. "He had no problem helping from behind the scenes," Limani said. "But he always wrote the check."

But isn't that what we expect from those who've been given so much? Locally, he wrote the checks, sometimes seven-figure ones, to benefit the school district, the hospital, the rec programs, the churches, and others who operate where the need is great. And he often insisted that such donations be given anonymously. Perhaps the true Palmer spirit was a million little gestures that brightened lives and gave encouragement to the sick or the sad. He felt, Rusbosin said, we are all capable of doing the little things to brighten the world. But he and his inspired staff and their networks of associates made it their mission to make those gestures.

Rusbosin knows firsthand. His father was living in Las Vegas in 2005 when he suffered a stroke. He knew Palmer, his son said, but it wasn't like they were buddies. But that relationship was far from his mind as he and his 10 siblings were going through the logistics of traveling west to comfort their loved one. "I get out there three days after we'd heard. I walk into the room in this nursing facility," Rusbosin said. "And the first thing I see on the board above his bed was a personal get-well letter to my dad from Arnold Palmer. How it got there before we did I'll never know."

He attributes the Palmer culture that instinctively knew how small gestures could make a big difference. "You wouldn't believe the care they gave my father," he said. "Doctors and nurses kept coming in all day to look at the letter and just see how he was doing. They were just enamored with him. He was the patient who was pals with Arnold Palmer."

The Palmer spirit means showing up even at times and places where you'd be excused for skipping. Dick Baumgardner, Latrobe Senior High class of '69, was there for one of them during one bitter cold December evening during the holiday season of 1968. He was a standout senior on the golf team that was the best in the county. It coincided with the season that the Wildcats also were among the best in the state.

The golfers were feeling slighted so Baumgardner and some friends organized a surprise awards banquet for coach Robert Cook. An invitation for Palmer to attend and present was proffered and accepted. He said he'd be there. "But we all read in the [Latrobe] *Bulletin* how a close elderly relation of his had died. Palmer would likely miss to be with his loved ones at the funeral home," Baumgardner said. "Plus the flu was going around, and a lot of people were staying in to avoid exposure."

But even virulent flu is no match for the spirit of Palmer. He'd left the funeral early to honor his commitment to Coach Cook and the kids. "He had three or four good excuses to blow us off, but he showed up, presented the award, greeted every guest, and just put a real exclamation point on our whole season," Baumgardner said. "It's something I'll never forget."

The Palmer spirit sometimes means feeling a moral obligation to all the time be aw-shucks-nice. Rob Herald says he feels it as he zooms around the globe as an international counselor for American Schools. He's resided for large chunks of the past 15 years in Cairo, Bangkok, Hong Kong, Tokyo, and is currently living in Dubai.

He was in Fort Worth, Texas, in the 1980s working with Big Brothers and Sisters when Palmer came to promote a local fund-raiser. The line to meet Palmer was long, but that didn't deter Herald. He got in it. "When my turn came, I said, 'Mr. Palmer, my name is Rob Herald, and I am also from Latrobe. I was friends with your daughter, Peggy, when we were in junior high.' Immediately his demeanor softened. It was like just hearing the name Latrobe put him in a whole different zone. We talked a little about Latrobe, and then he said, 'Have you ever played Latrobe Country Club?' I told him I never had and that I'd grown up caddying and playing public courses, and that Latrobe Elks was my home."

Palmer asked if he'd be home anytime soon. He'd be home that summer, Herald said.

"He said, 'Well, I want you to call Doc Giffin, and he will arrange for you to bring a foursome out to play the Country Club.' I was floored," Herald said. "After about a week, I called Giffin, and, sure enough, Arnie had told him I would be calling, and the game was arranged. What a kind and fantastic gesture from hometown boy to hometown boy.

He says the Palmer spirit lives on in him when he's counseling students in far off lands. He knows he might be the only American some of them will ever meet and he takes being a good example to heart. When he's not working, he enjoys playing golf, watching baseball, and spending time meeting with people at foreign prisons. "Some of these people feel truly godforsaken," he said. "My visits are more spiritual than religious. It's just my way of trying to give someone who needs it a ray of hope. I swear, it all comes from being raised in Latrobe. It's always had those core American values about giving back and helping others."

Herald always visits prisoners from other nations because it is his small effort to show what he believes America really is—compassionate, good-hearted, and providing a ray of hope in an often dark world. "I do believe they are surprised an American would take time to visit a stranger, but they are always very appreciative of the time and attention," Herald said. "In Egypt, the Somalian made me a really ornate name plate in the prison wood shop. They're very grateful and wind up having a much better—and more accurate—image of what America really means."

What's he plan on doing when he's done spending time in overseas

From left to right, Fuzzy Zoeller, Arnold Palmer, Lee Trevino, and Gary Player attend Palmer's 1995 gala, which raised money for the Arnold Palmer Hospital for Children. *(Howdy Giles)*

prisons? He's coming home to Latrobe. "It is just a special place," he said. "Everything I am today I am because I was raised in Latrobe. After my mom passed, I bought the family house so I can come home every summer. It's where I hope to wind up after I've seen enough of the world."

More often than not, the Palmer spirit would manifest itself in a letter like the one he'd written Len Vadas, a 1960 Latrobe graduate who met Palmer when the legendary golfer attended a sports banquet where Vadas and his football team were being honored. A true fan, Vadas would send Palmer holiday greeting cards, not an uncommon gesture by fans.

In 1998 Vadas was diagnosed with prostate cancer, one year after Palmer famously and successfully battled the same condition. During Vadas' treatment, his wife found a letter postmarked Youngstown, Pennsylvania, in the mail. "It was from Mr. Palmer," he said. "I opened it up and immediately started to cry. It was a personal letter encouraging me to keep fighting."

The letter reads: "I was very sorry to learn from [office secretary] Gina [Varrone] that you've been diagnosed with prostate cancer, but it is good to know they caught it early. I understand the tremendous emotions you're going through, but trust your operation will turn out as well as mine. Although the recuperation seems like an eternity, it wasn't long before I was back on the golf course. I wish you a speedy recovery and a return to the golf course, playing better than ever. Best wishes, Arnold Palmer."

Vadas fully recovered. He said he later reached out to Gina to thank her for her role in the correspondence. "She told me no one will ever know just how much he's always done for people," he said. "She said it was unbelievable."

The courtesy didn't have to involve life-threatening illness. It could be extended to more ordinary things like peaches. Michael Zart, also coincidentally of York, Pennsylvania, was friends with Kurt Kay, who was the son of Dick Kay, a former Latrobe Country Club member. In 1988 Dick moved his family to York to grow peaches at Brown's Orchards. "Dick did this every year religiously until he passed away in 2011," Zart said.

At that point Kurt and his other brother, Craig, continued the tradition that was so cherished that Winnie Palmer would call Kurt and ask when the peaches were coming. "I always marveled and begged him when I would be allowed to tag along since my in-laws lived down the street in Ligonier," Zart said. "As luck may have it, his older brother shared that he would be unable to attend the delivery the evening before, so Kurt asked me last minute, and I said 'Absolutely! When do we leave?'"

The answer was August 11, 2016. They knew Palmer was in failing health and steeled themselves to the realization this could be their last trip. They were greeted like family and even invited to join Arnold Palmer, Jerry Palmer, and Giffin for lunch in the club Grille Room. "After lunch he thanked us graciously, gave us gifts, and thanked us for coming," Zart said. "At that point, heading back to York, we both looked at each other that this very well may be the last time we ever see him. We marveled on his gracious disposition to others and felt very privileged to cherish this moment, as we knew in our heart of hearts that his days were short."

The famous courtesy even extended beyond Palmer's passing. Zart said he was shocked on January 27, 2017, to get a package from an address that excited and surprised him. Varrone explained their pictures had been found in Palmer's desk signed and dated the day Palmer left for Shadyside Hospital in Pittsburgh where he would die the next day. So perhaps The King's last official act before being whisked away was a gesture of thanks to some relative strangers to graciously thank them for some peaches.

Palmer's Dentist

Jimmy Bryan was 13 when Arnold Palmer became his idol. It was 1971, and he'd attended a Palmer exhibition at Statler's, a local recreational institution that through the years has featured a driving range, a par-3, mini-golf, go-carts, and batting cages. Statler's Fun Center is a staple of small-town summer fun. Forty years ago, Palmer used to stop by to mingle and grow the game of golf. It took root with Bryan. "I was at this really impressionable age, a young golfer, and here's the world's biggest golfer showing up at the local range to hit balls and say hello," he said. "He just had so much charisma and, man, he could hit the ball a mile. I remember thinking, *I want to be that guy.*"

Bryan was 17 when Palmer assumed another role— a neighborhood friend's father. He'd knock on the door to visit Amy Palmer, his classmate, and his idol would answer. It was jarring. What was this famous professional golfer doing at his friend's house? He initially had trouble processing that his idol was also his neighbor. Within a few years, his friend's father was writing letters of recommendation that would help him secure Tony Lema golf scholarships that paid one-third of Bryan's yearly tuition.

At the age of 27, Bryan had just become a dentist, and his friend Amy's mother, Winnie, asked if she could become his patient. Certainly, he said. Her initial appointments must have gone smoothly because she soon asked if he could peek into her husband's mouth. And, by the way, have you ever played golf with him?

Just like that, his iconic idol had become both his patient and golf partner. The steadfast friendship between the two happened almost as quickly. "I'll never forget the first time we golfed," he said. "I was nervous as hell. We set the match on the first tee. He gave me 8 strokes. I end up shooting a 79. He shoots 69, and I give him $50. He asks if I want to play tomorrow. I said sure. That day I shot 73, and he shoots 63. I gave him another $50 and said, 'Now, don't call me to play tomorrow!'"

He did call and he called again the day after that. In fact, he never stopped calling, and Bryan went on to became the man who for 30 years played more golf with Palmer than perhaps anyone on earth. And Bryan played in the age when Palmer was most grand, or what philosophers call "a man in full."

Bryan rode the cart with him during the watershed moments of Palmer's later life, including his '97 cancer diagnosis, the '99 passing of his first wife, and for all the births of their grandchildren. Their conversational topics included the O.J. Simpson trial, the 9/11 attacks, Deflategate, Tonya Harding, the iPhone, steroids in baseball, Princess Di. Anything that you talked about during your rounds with your golf buddies over the last three decades he talked about with his. Only one of his was Arnold Palmer.

And if Bryan wanted to know what Muhammed Ali or Clint Eastwood or Donald Trump or Queen Elizabeth was really like, he could just ask. "About 10 years into it, it began to dawn on me that we'd become truly good friends," he said. "I was always fully aware of his stardom and my enormous admiration for him, but those barriers were all down. I knew he'd be there for me, and he knew I'd be there for him. We were very close."

He knew his friend was struggling when Winnie passed. He did what friends do. "He was being overwhelmed," Bryan said. "I made it a point to get him away. I got him in a cart, and we rode out to No. 15, just the two of us. There was no one else on the course."

And there together, the two friends wept a good long, healing cry. The flip side was a lot of uproarious laughter amidst profound lessons on life. Palmer, he said, had a sublime gift for making every person in his presence become convinced he or she was the most important person he'd ever met—even an obvious fraud.

Bryan remembered the time a stranger approached them on the roadside No. 2 green. He was wearing black pants, a blue sport coat, and a blue shirt that had a ratty old index card folded up by the top button where a traditional priest would have a clerical collar. "The guy's mildly disheveled, and he interrupts as we're putting and says, 'Mr. Palmer, I'm Father So-and-So and I'm hoping you'd sign these 20 Masters flags to help the orphans.' Well, Arnold looks at him and looks at me and back at the guy."

Palmer said he didn't have time to sign them all. Bryan said he signed about five, shook the father's hand, and immediately went back to lining up his putt as Father So-and-So hightailed it down the road. "We finally say, 'C'mon, that guy's clearly a phony,'" Bryan said. "'Why'd you sign his flags? You know he's just gonna sell them on the Internet.'"

Palmer got an innocent look on his face and said, "What? The guy's a priest! I can't say no to a man of the cloth!"

But there were plenty of perks of being Palmer's friend. There was the time he flew him, Marty Newingham, and Brian Miller—Palmer's rock solid foursome during his last 10 years—to play Augusta and had them join him in the champion's locker room for drinks and hors d'oeuvres. How exclusive was the venue? Members like Bill Gates and Warren Buffet have never been in there.

If Palmer felt like playing Pine Valley, Pebble Beach, or somewhere else exclusive, he'd summon Jimmy, Marty, and Brian, and they'd be on their way. One of his favorite memories was when Palmer took the men to Oakmont and on every hole gave a precise breakdown of what happened on the fabled course in the '62 and '73 U.S. Opens. "His recall was perfect," he said. "He wasn't bitter. He was just telling us what happened. It was like living through this history inside his head. It's something I'll never forget."

What kind of patient was his good friend? "He was a good patient," he said. "He took good care of his teeth. He understood the importance of his smile. I remember one time he was getting his partial denture adjusted, and he shows up in my lab and started grinding away at it. It was like he was working on his clubs in his own workshop. He took good care of his smile."

And it took good care of him. Bryan said Palmer once asked if he should maybe whiten the ivories, add some dazzle. He was worried his smile was becoming dingy. "I said, 'Arnold, your smile is one of the most popular smiles on the planet,'" he said. "'We're not doing anything that might change that.' He said, 'You're right.' His teeth were important, but he knew what really mattered was the authenticity of that wonderful smile."

Bryan was 13 when Palmer became his idol. He was 17 when he became his scholarship sponsor. He was 27 when he became his dentist and golf partner. And he was 58 when he lost him. "I miss him every single day. I realize just how very blessed I was to know one person—any person—who was that kind, that much fun, and that accepting of people and all their flaws," Bryan said. "He would put his arm around you, and you could truly feel his love. You knew you really meant something to him. You knew you mattered to him. Everyone did. We're all lucky to have even one special person like that in our lives, and with me that one special person just happened to be Arnold Palmer."

Chapter 11

Jerry Palmer

Born 15 years after his brother, Jerry Palmer then died on November 19, 2016, just 55 days after Arnold Palmer. He was 72. His once zesty mental acuities had been in decline for years. It was a real pity because he was one of the most joyful men I've ever known. It seemed so unfair.

Jerry was simultaneously the worst golfer and the sweetest guy I've ever known. The two rarely equate. Bad golfers throw clubs; Jerry threw parties. When people would ask me about the differences between the brothers, I had a handy answer: Arnold was approachable, Jerry was unavoidable. Whether it was The Tin Lizzy, the Palmer hotel, or the Touchdown Club, Jerry was there—sometimes all on the same night. "He was always a lot of fun," said attorney Chuck Mason, a longtime friend. "He was very comfortable in his brother's shadow. They were alike in how they treated people, didn't matter if it was a CEO or the guys on the maintenance crew. Arnold's charisma was known around the world, and Jerry was very humble, caring, and self-deprecating, just a great, great guy who truly cared for his friends, and sooner or later, everyone became his friend. And he did a wonderful job raising Deacon and Amanda as a single father. No, he couldn't golf, but he did all the big things very well."

I argue that Jerry was the only person on the planet who loved golf more than Arnold. Arnold's love of golf left him richly rewarded. From a young age, his achievements nurtured his love. Golf bestowed Arnold with wealth, adulation, and historic renown that will forever endure. If golf is a mistress, she succumbed to Arnold. She ridiculed Jerry, taunted his courtship, denied her comely affections. He didn't care. He never stopped loving her. There's real beauty in that.

Golfers love the older brother, but, man, most of us can really relate to the younger one. If golf was unkind to him, the number of people who enjoyed his presence—and he knew everyone—made up for it.

It was just so easy being nice to Jerry. The brother of The King was a real prince. I'd known him about 15 years and profiled him for *Kingdom Magazine* in 2008. The thrust of the article was: gee, what's it like growing up and living in the shadow of one of the world's most famous and beloved men? There are plenty of cases of resentful siblings who let residual fame warp them into dysfunction. It was never a problem with Jerry.

C'mon, I asked, wasn't being Arnold's brother ever a burden? "Honestly, I can't think of a single burden," he said. "I enjoy my life. I have two wonderful children, a job I love, and I have one of the world's biggest celebrities for a big brother, and the celebrity just happens to be a great guy in every way."

Then, I asked him to tell me about the perks. He rattled off just a few: chatting with presidents and first ladies during lavish ceremonies in the White House; becoming chummy with actors, athletes, and powerful businessmen and businesswomen from around the world; and getting to play the finest golf courses in the world. "Oh, and Arnold Palmer's your brother! Really, there hasn't been a time in my life when he wasn't a celebrity," Jerry said. "Even when I was a really little kid, he was always

Arnold Palmer was always close with his family. From left to right, Emily, Annie, Sam, Katie, Will, and Anna dine with their grandfather. *(Howdy Giles)*

getting headlines and honors for his golf. And, yeah, I idolized him. My ambition growing up was to get a job working for Arnold Palmer."

It was an ambition that was fulfilled through about 2012. Those who worked for him say he treated his staff like family. And nobody—even club members—were allowed to mess with Jerry's family, said Karen Ulischney, a former waitress at the club. "He was a very sweet man, but nobody was going to walk all over him," she said. "I remember one night where a couple of members had been drinking a lot and started mistreating some of the waitresses. The next day he really let them have it." He told staff that day they needed to come to Jerry anytime anyone got out of line.

I liked the time he told me his favorite memories of time spent with his brother weren't at the White House or some party crowded with A-listers. The best times, he said, were just the two of them at the practice range. "Usually, it's just the two of us," he said. "Sometimes we don't say much. But sometimes we talk about all the changes we've seen on that little piece of ground, the people we've known, and the places we've been. To be there with my brother, Arnold Palmer, and know how fulfilling our lives have been and how we're still happiest right there where we started is very special."

This man so imbued with grace and humility often told me how blessed he felt his life had been. "You see," he'd say, "I'm really a very lucky man. Sure, I wish my golf game was better. My brother's made a lifelong project out of me, but I always tell people the Palmers already have one fine golfer in the family. I enjoy being out there, but the game's frustrating."

While Jerry was always sunny, the memory of him I'll carry longest is one of meteorological misery. For years, Jerry, his insurance agent Ron Carmassi, and state trooper Steve Limani—his friendships were delightfully eclectic—and I would drive to Stonewall Resort in Roanoke, West Virginia, for golf and camaraderie. It was our year-end custom. He's played at many of the finest courses in the world but always said Stonewall was one of his favorites.

But on this day the forecast was discouraging. Day-long rains, bitter gusts, and descending temperatures were going on, and I argued we skip it in favor of what I was certain would be a long, boozy lunch near a roaring fire.

Jerry wouldn't hear of it. He was determined to uphold our tradition. I don't think I've ever been more miserable on a golf course. After one hole we were drenched and chilled to the bone. At the 9th hole, we had what you might consider a golfer's intervention. "Jerry, this is nuts," I said. "Let's quit. The bar's open!"

Jerry wouldn't hear of it: "I really think the weather's going to change. And why would we quit when we're all having so much fun?"

He was correct. The weather did change.

It got much worse. I remember being at the most distant point from the warmth of the clubhouse and in a driving rain seeing Jerry whiff again and again and again at a ball stuck in a difficult lie. And he looked like the happiest man in the world. Later at dinner he jabbed us for having wanted to quit. "Wasn't that fun?" he said. "Wasn't that just the greatest day?"

It was marvelous, just like Jerry. I imagine the sweet, smiling guy in heaven right now with the look of a man who'd known all along what to expect.

Chapter 12

Arnold Palmer Regional Airport

Holly Rutter Bush was nine years old before she learned the connection between the thunderous boom of the low-flying jet roaring just over her house and the sporty Cadillac that went racing past moments later. The Rutter family lived on Gravel Hill Road right between the Latrobe, Pennsylvania, airport and the home of a famous golfer. "I remember being outside with my mother, trimming a forsythia bush one spring day," she said. "I was used to hearing airplanes at all hours from Latrobe Airport, just up the road past Route 981, but this was different, closer, and sent a vibration down my arms and legs with its boom. Mom said, 'Arnie must be home.' I didn't think much of it even when a long car came past us in a hurry. The woman driving and my mother exchanged waves, and Mom said, 'There goes Winnie.'"

Her mom explained that Arnold Palmer flies low to let Winnie know that he's home and to come pick him up at the airport. Palmer later told Mrs. Rutter that Palmer always said he aimed at their house so he could come in low over his. Of course, this was a man who felt right at home in the cockpit. He made it clear that had he not excelled in golf he'd have found the same joy in aviation. "He loved everything about being at the airport and BS-ing with the pilots," said airport manager Gabe Monzo. "He especially loved the air show."

And he loved aviation. By the time he was 26, he'd decided that learning to fly his own plane would become an indispensable part of his success. The future golfing legend sought lessons from a man who'd teach more than 1,000 students how to fly at Latrobe, becoming a legend himself along the way. That aviation legend, Elias R. "Babe" Krinock, died in 2009 at the age of 85. I wrote a feature story about Babe in 2007.

A statue of Arnold Palmer graces the airport that bears his name in Latrobe, Pennsylvania. *(Chris Rodell)*

He told me all about his star pupil and his learning to fly on the single-engine Cessna 172. "After just four hours of flight time, he was saying, 'You know I can fly this thing by myself,'" Krinock said of Palmer. "So after six hours, I let him solo, took him two hours less than it took me. He brings it up every time he sees me. I tell him it's because he had the better instructor."

Obviously, the Arnold Palmer Regional Airport is full of Palmer memorabilia and stories of Palmer, the pilot, including one from 1972. Frank Harsh was among the most highly recruited athletes in the country. The two-sport Blairsville star (baseball and football) was sought by coaches at Notre Dame, Kentucky, and Minnesota. Most persuasive and persistent was Joe Paterno of the Penn State Nittany Lions. Paterno may have enjoyed home-field advantage, but he didn't have his own plane. "Mr. Palmer called my parents and said he wanted to fly me to Wake Forest to meet the coach," Harsh said. "It really impressed my parents—me, too. He was a legend and he wanted me to go play for his old school."

So did he wind up at Wake? "Sure did!" Harsh said. "I loved it there. And I love telling people the story of how Arnold Palmer recruited me with a flight on his private jet."

Circumstances were a little different for local businessman Lester Sutton, president of Aggressive Grinding. He was just along for the ride, but, oh, what a ride. It was 2011, and Sutton and his Uncle Ray were scrambling for Mother's Day weekend tickets to fly from Pittsburgh to Orlando, Florida, and Sutton was at the time looking at a two-hour drive to the Pittsburgh airport and expensive, short-notice airline rates. The sensible option was starting to look like making the 20-hour drive. He was explaining this to Palmer and his Grille Room lunchmates. Palmer turned to Sutton and said, "Well, we're flying to Orlando tomorrow. Why don't you join us?" Sutton's reaction: "I was dumbfounded," he said. "I didn't feel right just accepting such a generous offer so I started to mumble excuses. I told him it was very kind of him, but my Uncle Ray had already agreed to drive."

Palmer asked pilot Pete Luster if they had room for Uncle Ray. They did. It began to dawn on Sutton he wasn't going to take no for an answer. He felt compelled to make a gesture of appreciation. He said he'd like to chip in for fuel. "Son," Palmer said, "you'd better have some pretty big chips." And just like that, a 20-hour vehicular ordeal was transformed into a breezy little jaunt at 37,000 feet. Sutton said the flight took one hour and 37 minutes.

He attributes the impromptu offer to Palmer's eagerness to always help people who help people. Sutton had been serving as the chair of the local Red Cross. "If you were doing something in the community to help the community," Sutton said, "then Arnold Palmer knew about it."

Monzo's been a volunteer firefighter most of his life in a town where that really means something. It's a culture that respects selflessness, devotion, and daring in the face of life-threatening danger. And in that culture, the man most deserving of respect is the chief.

So Monzo never called Palmer, a man with whom he'd been friends for 40 years, Arnold, Arnie, or Arn. In formal situations, he'd occasionally call him Mr. Palmer. But this manager, as friendly, generous, and competent a man as any in Latrobe, called Palmer "Chief." "It was as true a term of endearment as any I could use for this great man. It was such a privilege for me to have him in my life," Monzo said. "Sometimes, nearly a year later, it still seems like a dream."

Chapter 13

The Palmer Timeline

It was in 2006 when a prominent Pittsburgh sportscaster declared Arnold Palmer's announcement that he'd be retiring from tournament golf meant it was "a momentous day in the life of the Latrobe golfer." But in the grand scheme of things, it was fairly insignificant.

By then I had immersing myself for nearly a year in what a truly momentous day meant in the life of Palmer. I'd been given a crash course in understanding how a truly momentous day for me and you differed from one for Palmer. Our momentous days usually involve scattered anniversaries, birthdays, or, perhaps, a date of occupational significance.

It's different with Palmer. For him, something worthy of festive recollection happened every single day of the year. Take June 23. That was when President George W. Bush bestowed upon him the Presidential Medal of Honor (2004), nearly 11 years after Palmer was still basking over being honored by President Bill Clinton with the first National Sports Award (1993). Those prestigious honors kind of make winning the 1985 Senior T.P.C. Championship (also June 23) and earning $36,554 seem like small potatoes.

Or July 29, Palmer won three tournaments in three decades in

Arnold Palmer, who was inducted into the Wake Forest Sports Hall of Fame on September 25, 1971, poses with former Demon Deacons coach, Jesse Haddock. (*Howdy Giles*)

three different states for an escalating first place prize of $3,800 (1956), $11,000 (1963), and $20,050 (1971). I knew all this because Palmer's personal assistant, Doc Giffin, had spent the previous 40 years methodically scissoring every single newspaper and magazine article that mentioned the boss' name and putting the clippings in stacked boxes in the basement of their Latrobe, Pennsylvania, office. I'd been asked by ArnoldPalmer.com in 2005 to go through the boxes and assemble a day-by-day timeline of Palmer's life.

As everyone knew, he was one of the greatest golfers who'd ever lived. But a charming alchemy of small-town grit, old-fashioned good manners, and heaven-sent good fortune have made his a life unique in American history. Many presidents may admire Sandy Koufax or Cal Ripken, but that doesn't mean they'll ever invite them to the White House to play catch.

But it's different with golfers. And it was different still with Palmer. That helps explain why former President Dwight D. Eisenhower showed up at Palmer's house in Latrobe on September 10, 1966, to surprise him on his 37th birthday and why former President Gerald R. Ford's first act as a private citizen on January 20, 1977, was to fly to Pebble Beach to golf with Palmer. Clinton told biographers in 2000 that one of the greatest perks of being president of the United States is the "opportunity to play golf with Arnold Palmer."

It was a Palmer team—him and wife Kit—that on May 7, 2007, made one of the most selective cuts of the 21st century. They were among the 130 A-list guests invited to fete Queen Elizabeth II at the White House, a truly regal white tie affair considered by society writers at *The Washington Post* to be the most spectacular and lavish dinner hosted by an official in Washington in more than a decade. Palmer's name on the guest list added a dash of grit and grace to a roll that included Vice President Dick Cheney, Nancy Reagan, Peyton Manning, and violinist Itzhak Perlman.

Amazingly enough, it was Palmer's second state dinner. His first was May 14, 1991, when President George H.W. Bush honored the queen. The only guests who were at both regal affairs 16 years apart? Queen Elizabeth, Prince Philip, and Palmer.

I was tickled to think about how future Palmer biographers would feast on the tasty leftovers from the following day when Palmer was up early giving putting lessons to a trio of renown rules sticklers who might be hiding snazzy golf shirts beneath their black robes. The Palmers had accepted the invitation of U.S. Supreme Court Justice Anthony Kennedy, a friend of Kit's, to visit the highest court in the land. Spying Palmer there, Chief Justice John Roberts put down his gavel and picked up his putter. "He was putting on the carpet in Chief Justice Roberts' office and giving some pointers to Roberts, Kennedy, and former Justice Sandra Day O'Connor, who, incidentally, is the only Supreme Court Justice to ever score a hole in one," Giffin said.

But the coolest coda to this fairytale is that the Palmers left Washington and immediately flew to Bay Hill Club in Orlando, so Palmer could do one of the few things he enjoys more than dining with royalty. He golfed with friends.

Scrutiny of some of his more esoteric golf records yielded thrilling results—not yet divined by any of the multitude of sportswriters or the most ardent Palmer fans. For instance, on November 23, 1987, Palmer revealed that golf buddy and former San Francisco Giants owner Bob Lurie offered him a one-year contract to manage his listless baseball team. Palmer declined. "Not enough money," he said.

Clips from March 3, 2004, told how Palmer and New York Yankees manager Joe Torre were on a Hawaiian whale-watching cruise when Palmer shamed Torre, then 64, out of thoughts of retiring. "He said, 'Hey, I'm 74 and I'm never going to retire,'" said Torre, recalling Palmer's scold. Fourteen years later Torre remains engaged in day-to-day operations with Major League Baseball.

As an admiring student of legendary sportswriters, I reveled in clips from titans like Jim Murray giving their unique take on Palmer. There was this nugget from the August 26, 1969, edition of the *Los Angeles Times*: "Arnold Palmer plays golf as if he were fighting a lion. It's him or it. He's never hit a timid shot in his life. They haven't made a golf hole that could scare Palmer. He could par 42nd Street if he ever made up his mind to do it. Arnold leaving golf is like a 2000-year-old Redwood toppling. It is Napoleon going to Elba, Caesar falling, declining. After him, it's the Dark Ages."

Murray didn't know it then, but thanks to Palmer's crucial

involvement in the Senior Tour, colleagues would still be saluting Palmer's competitive muscle nearly 20 years later. This was from March 29, 1987, when Scott Ostler sought to identify the biggest hotdog in sports. Was it Reggie Jackson? John McEnroe? Hulk Hogan? Nope, he said. It was Palmer. "He's the biggest, hands down," Ostler wrote. "To qualify for hotdog status, one must: 1. Have an exciting game, a flair, a unique style; 2. Play to the crowd; 3. Enjoy the spotlight. Nowhere does it say a hotdog has to be a jerk, although many are. Arnie is not a pants dropper. He is a pants hitcher. He still uses that simple tug of the belt to convey the message, 'Excuse me, gentlemen, but this is Arnold Palmer's golf tournament.'"

Other nuggets from Doc's meticulous clippings include:

- The James Bond movie *Goldfinger* was released in America on December 22, 1964. In the film an incredulous caddie speculates the arch-villain is cheating by sarcastically telling Sean Connery as Bond: "If that's his original ball, I'm Arnold Palmer."

- Palmer smoked his last cigarette on December 23, 1973. The man whose first major endorsement was for L&M Cigarettes said there were 16 people at the party, and they were all smoking. "We decided that if any of us ever smoked another cigarette, we had to give $100 to the 15 other people—not just for that night but for the rest of our lives," he said. "Right there it stopped me."

- A faded yellow clip has "1960" on it, but no other date from the interview when famed designer Oleg Cassini weighed in on the Palmer phenomenon: "He's totally inelegant. If his pants fit, he wouldn't have to hitch them up all the time." Trade publications from 1966, however, show that six years later, Arnold Palmer sportswear began outselling Cassini items at Macy's in New York.

There were reams of clips generated from the aviation world record Palmer set May 19, 1976, when he circumnavigated the globe in a Learjet 36 in less than 58 hours and his enduring love of aviation. His endorsements, his celebrity friendships (Kirk Douglas said in 1970 that no one—not Sinatra, John Wayne, or Ronald Reagan—has more charisma than Palmer), the more than 250 courses he's designed in 20 countries, the hospitals he's opened, the lives he's touched are staggering.

Here is a month-by-month timeline of that incredible life.

JANUARY 2

2007

Wake Forest Demon Deacon Arnold Palmer and Louisville-native Muhammad Ali served as honorary captains representing their teams and towns at the Orange Bowl in Miami. The Louisville Cardinals won 24–13.

1988

Palmer assistant Doc Giffin revealed many people thought he was crazy for taking the Palmer job in 1966. "They said, 'His career's almost over. Why take a job with no future?' But with his business activities, golf course design, and involvement in the Senior Tour, he'll always need me."

JANUARY 6

1961

Palmer took, yikes, a 12 on the 508-yard 9th hole at the Rancho Park Golf Course during the 1961 Los Angeles Open after blasting four straight balls out of bounds. Club members were so amazed that the defending U.S. Open and Masters champion could take a 7-over-par that they installed a plaque commemorating the deed. The plaque is still there today. When asked later how the great Arnold Palmer could card a 12, Palmer replied, "It was easy. I missed a 30-foot putt for an 11.

JANUARY 9
1966

Palmer shot 72-66-62-73-273 for what *Golf World* called a 3-stroke statement victory: "As he stood on the 18th green of Rancho Municipal [Golf Course] with the Los Angeles Open winner's check of $11,000 in his big mitts, his first thought must have been, 'Okay, everybody off my back now. I've won again, and my putting was fine.' In recent years he had been so involved in related business that tournaments got the short end of his attention, to which he admits. His price of popularity has been incessant advice, in public and private, on how to end his 'slump.'"

1961

Palmer was awarded the coveted Sportsman of the Year by *Sports Illustrated*. The 25-cent magazine said it chose Palmer "for dominating the game of golf with a bold determination while adding to its splendor with genuine graciousness and charm." The accompanying profile said, "while his daring comes out on the golf course, in stunting airplanes and in an expensive taste for cars, he also has a very conservative streak. Winnie is not permitted to wear fingernail polish, dyed hair is anathema, and when he built his house three years ago, it was too small because he insisted on paying for it with cash."

JANUARY 12
1962

Legendary golfer Walter Hagen gave *Esquire* magazine his take on Palmer: "I used to say I didn't want to be a millionaire. I just wanted to live like one. It looks like this Palmer fellow is going to get to do both. He's great. He plays with skill, imagination, and courage. I believe he is the greatest champion of the day and in golf the greatest of the great. His most significant remark, to me, is 'I get no enjoyment out of the game unless the pressure is on,' indicates to me why he is a strong finisher like I was. If I were in my prime today and had to play him, I'd find some reason to be out of town."

JANUARY 22

1977

The majority of a record gallery estimated at 25,000 total saw Palmer playing partner Gerald Ford chip in on the 14th hole at Pebble Beach during the Bing Crosby Pro-Am. Palmer said, "I told him, 'Let's show 'em a little class, Mr. President.' He said, 'Wouldn't it be something if I made this?' And darned if he didn't proceed to chip it in." When someone joked that if all the people following him and Palmer had voted for Ford, he'd still be president, Ford said, "Yes, but then I wouldn't be playing here today either."

1950

Still reeling over the death of close friend and Wake Forest golf teammate Bud Worsham, Arnold Palmer enlisted in the U.S. Coast Guard and reported in 1950 to a base in Cape May, New Jersey. The athletic Palmer was surprised to learn he almost didn't qualify because he had flat feet. Years of running barefoot across Latrobe Country Club had taken a toll. Palmer, however, passed the physicals and was soon serving a three-year stint.

JANUARY 24

1995

The *South China Morning Post* reported Palmer and Philippine President Fidel Ramos enjoyed a friendly round during the grand opening of the Orchard Golf and Country Club near Manila. The Palmer Design course was set to host the Johnnie Walker Classic later that week. Palmer pronounced himself "extremely pleased" with the course.

1960

Palmer won the prestigious Hickok Belt as the popular men's sportswear manufacturer's "Professional Athlete of the Year." Palmer and other top athletes shared an elevator ride to the awards ceremony, causing Roger Maris to look around, see Palmer, and say, "What the hell are you doing here?" Palmer later accepted the New York Yankee's congratulations on winning.

JANUARY 25

1991

Palmer's business endeavors were so lucrative that a lengthy *USA TODAY* profile said that for years Palmer had been losing money every time he played in a tournament—even when he won "because he could make more than that at an outing or a speaking engagement."

1959

Palmer shot a final round 62—the low round for the year—to win the Thunderbird Invitational at the Thunderbird Country Club in Rancho Mirage, California. He earned $1,500. It was his 13th victory since joining the PGA Tour in 1955.

JANUARY 31

1968

Palmer explained how he dealt with disruptive and boisterous crowds in a game that's best observed in silence: "Sure, it's tough when the crowds get going. You can't concentrate. But you get to the point where you start to expect anything—noise, shoving, cameras clicking, people grinding, and pulling on your arm wanting something. But meeting and talking to people is my whole life. I genuinely like people, so it's not going to bother me."

FEBRUARY 4

1971

The *Orlando Sentinel* profiled Arnold Palmer assistant Doc Giffin about the long-term prospects for his job. "Oh, I view it as a lifetime job. When Arnold's playing days are over, he'll still be in tremendous demand as a speaker and so on. Meanwhile, he thinks and I think, that he's got a lot of tournament wins left in him." In the article Giffin laid to rest the myth that being associated with a great golfer necessarily made him a great golfer. "The truth is I've never had a round below 82 in my life, and on a course like Bay Hill, I'm lucky to break 100."

1968

Palmer beat Deane Beman in a two-hole playoff to win the Bob Hope Desert Classic and $20,000. On hand to congratulate him were former President Dwight D. Eisenhower and future president, California Governor Ronald Reagan. The win caused the *Greensboro News-Record* to note it was Palmers 52nd win in 14 years and "gives rise to the belief that Palmer is again embarking on another brilliant year."

1962

Palmer won the Palm Springs Classic and earned $5,300.

FEBRUARY 12

1961

Palmer earned $4,300 after placing first at the Phoenix Open at Arizona Country Club.

FEBRUARY 14

1986

Palmer and assembled dignitaries broke ground for the Arnold Palmer Hospital for Children in Orlando, Florida.

1971

Palmer ended a 14-month victory drought by sinking an 18-foot birdie putt on the first sudden death playoff hole against Ray Floyd to win the Bob Hope Desert Classic. While Hope was presenting Palmer with the $28,000 winner's check, a man named Robert Zirbes stormed the ceremony and began waving a putter and shouting, "It was fixed! It was fixed, and I can prove it!" He was wrestled to the ground and taken away. Palm Springs police later revealed he'd started the tournament as Orville Moody's caddie, but Moody dismissed him after the Saturday round. No reason was given. Asked to comment about the fix charge, a weary Palmer replied, "I just wish to hell someone would have told me. It would have saved me about 15 pounds and 150 gray hairs." The ceremony resumed, and Vice President Spiro Agnew presented Palmer with the Eisenhower Trophy.

1969

The Palmers visited President Dwight Eisenhower at Walter Reed Hospital for conversation, coffee, and heart-shaped cookies.

"Gosh, it's great to see you kids!" Eisenhower exclaimed. Topics of discussion included golf, politics, the Vietnam War, children, grandchildren, and pointed questions about if Palmer was ever going to quit smoking. It was the last time the friends were together before Eisenhower passed away on March 28.

MARCH 1

1978

In advance of the Florida Citrus Open, Palmer took reporters and fellow golf pros on a cross-town tour at his Bay Hill Club and said he envisioned a day when the "tournament-ready" course would serve as a regular stop on the PGA Tour or, perhaps, the U.S. Open championship.

1960

Palmer won the 1960 Texas Open and earned $2,800 at the Fort Sam Houston Golf Course.

MARCH 4

1975

"What's the best tip you can give to a weekend golfer?" That was among the questions Palmer said he'd been asked most. His answer: "Get to the course early enough to loosen up and hit a few balls before you tee off. If you only play once or twice a week, those muscles need loosening up before you start. Otherwise, you'll waste a few holes of the round before you get loose."

1969

Hal Winkler, president of Executive Securities Corporation, paid $49,000 more than the usual $1,000 entry fee at the Doral Open Pro-Am to ensure he'd play his round with Palmer. Tournament director Paul Warren said the rules stipulate a blind draw for pros and amateurs, "However, if a man gives $50,000 and wants to play with Arnie, we'll make an exception to the rules." The money was a windfall for American Cancer Society.

MARCH 6

1977

At the request of the *Orlando Sentinel-Star*, former New York Yankees pitcher and *Ball Four* author Jim Bouton wrote about Palmer: "I took a lot of heat for writing in *Ball Four* that Mickey Mantle and Roger Maris were often rude to fans and reporters. It was argued that they're pestered all the time so they were entitled to be rude. Well, Arnold Palmer is pestered more than anybody, yet he manages to be nice to people—even when he's under pressure."

1960

Palmer won $2,000 at the Baton Rouge Open championship at the Baton Rouge Country Club. Years later, Palmer joked that the abundance of all the $2,000 purses he won as a young man were the reason he worked so hard as an old man.

MARCH 7

1988

Palmer prophetically told reporters, "I see the day, not too far distant, when every tournament will have at least a $1 million purse. Eventually, they'll have to have a second tour for the younger golfers."

1959

Palmer was asked if he'd ever been fretful about the outcome of an unlikely shot. He responded: "When I take a shot that seems bold, it never occurs to me that I might miss it. And when I do, I'm surprised as hell. I can't believe it."

MARCH 12
2006

The *Peoria (Illinois) Journal Star* published a full-page article headlined, "Big-League Devotion" about sports memorabilia collectors like Ron Ames whose dedication to collecting Palmer items began in 1990 when he cashed in a profit-sharing check for $1,350, borrowed another $500, and bought a $1,850 statue of Palmer. Since then, his obsession for Palmer memorabilia has overtaken a spare bedroom and includes 200 Palmer autographed items and autographs from Palmer's grandson, Sam Saunders, and his dentist, Palmer memorabilia collector extraordinaire, Howdy Giles.

1971

Mike Bradley, 16, of Winter Park, Florida, followed Palmer during his second round at the Florida Citrus Invitational and earned a meeting with Palmer after telling reporters he counted the golfer hitching up his pants 345 times during the round. Local newspapers ran a picture headlined, "'Hitcher' Meets 'Counter,'" in which Palmer explained, "The reason I hitch my trousers goes back to a time when I was about your age. My hips were always sort of narrow and had a tendency to slide down. My mother was always on me about it," he grinned, "saying, 'Arnold, tuck your shirttail in.' So in order to please her, I started pulling 'em up all the time. I've done it so long that I'm totally unconscious of even doing it."

MARCH 17

1994

Palmer broke personal precedent and charged a fee for his autograph. Told that business at his grandchildren's 18th hole lemonade stand was slow, Palmer took time out from his hosting duties at Bay Hill and agreed to sign autographs for anyone who'll buy a $1.50 glass of lemonade. Thirty minutes later, the stand closed after taking in $50 and running dry of lemonade.

1993

On the eve of the Bay Hill Invitational, Palmer and Jack Nicklaus regaled reporters with stories of their legendary rivalry. "I always, every day, looked to see what he shot," Palmer said. To which Nicklaus replied, "Me, too. Still do. When I pick up the paper, I still look to see where Palmer is."

1902

Robert Tyre Jones was born on this day. His legacy and instruction books carried great meaning for Palmer. "Jones brought the game of golf to the world's attention. His books were the first ones I read about golf and about his prowess and that left a lasting impression on me," Palmer said.

MARCH 18

2002

Principal Harry Beil read what he called an "inspirational" letter from Palmer at a high school assembly on driving safety after the school tragically lost eight students to accidents during the 2001–02 school year.

1969

In a United Press International profile of Palmer, the reporter wrote about the volume of letters from soldiers serving in Vietnam. "One says, 'Dear Mr. Palmer, I have a favor to ask of you, sir. Please do not retire from the game of golf. I've been playing many years and have learned a lot just by watching you on TV. I know you cannot go on forever, but you retiring would be like Willie Mays leaving baseball. The game wouldn't be the same. I come home in February and wouldn't be able to stand watching a tournament if you're not in it.'"

1968

The Pittsburgh Press reported Palmer got 40 to 50 fan letters every day—unless he won. Then the total zoomed up to as high as 200 letters a day.

APRIL 4

1995

Augusta National honored Palmer by dedicating a plaque to him next to a newly constructed water fountain near the 16th tee. The four-time Masters champ was only the fourth player ever so honored. The others were Gene Sarazen, Byron Nelson, and Ben Hogan. Palmer birdied the hole the next two days of the tournament but missed the cut.

1968

Cartoonist Charles M. Schulz began a six-day salute to Palmer and The Masters by depicting Snoopy accepting an invitation to play in the tournament, flying his "private jet" (doghouse) to Georgia, grinning, and saying, "I'll probably stay with Arnold and Winnie!"

APRIL 7

1983

Palmer shot an opening round 68 at Augusta. It was his best round in the last year that he made the cut of a tournament he'd won four times.

1962

Sports Illustrated writer Ray Cave advised Palmer on what shirt to wear during the last round of The Masters so he'd stand out on the cover of the magazine.

APRIL 8

1993

Palmer, 63, created goose bumps on all of Arnie's Army by birdieing the first three holes to jump to the top of the Augusta leader board. The four-time Masters champ wound up shooting a 74. He told reporters, "I started good, finished good, but died in the middle. The good news, I guess, is I made five birdies. The bad news is I made a lot more bogeys."

1962

In what many newspapers called "The Shot Heard 'Round the World," Palmer sunk a 45-foot birdie chip shot from the left fringe of the 16th green at Augusta. The shot resembled in trajectory and roll the one Tiger Woods would hit on his way to winning the 2005 Masters. Palmer's shot set up a three-way tie for first that concluded Monday when he beat Gary Player and Dow Finsterwald for his third green jacket. Bob Jones told him, "Your courage, skill, and stamina are unmatchable. I have the most extravagant admiration for you both as a person and as a player."

1960

Troubled by a blister during the second round at Augusta, Palmer soldiered on by slipping a torn scorecard in his shoe. He shot 73 on his way to his second Masters victory.

APRIL 10

2005

Tiger Woods sunk one of the most dramatic chips in golf on the 16th hole at Augusta on his way to winning his fourth green jacket. Announcer Verne Lundquist said, "Oh, wow! In your life have you ever seen anything like that?" Knowledgeable golf fans nodded yes and thought of Palmer in 1962. Palmer told reporters, "I was sitting in my living room describing it to my wife. I told her I had been in that same position. Mine was a little higher. [Golfer Jimmy] Demaret was up in the tower, and I could hear him saying, 'If Palmer gets this up and down, it'll be a miracle. It's really difficult, and the green is really fast'—all those adjectives. I wanted to look up at him and tell him, 'Just hold on a minute.' I pitched it, and it rolled down, much the same as Tiger's did. It didn't have the same break, but the pin was almost in an identical position. And I won the tournament."

1983

Palmer finished The Masters tied for 36th after rounds of 68-74-76-78. It was the last year he played all four rounds of the tournament.

1961

Palmer disappointed his army of fans by making a confounding double bogey on the 18th green to lose the 1961 Masters by 1 stroke. Palmer stopped to chat with a friend along the fairway who told him, "Nice going, boy. You won it." Palmer later acknowledged making a "huge" mistake by prematurely accepting the congratulations that destroyed his concentration. He tied with venerable amateur Charlie Coe and allowed Gary Player to win his first green jacket.

1960

Announcer Jim McKay's excited chatter in the booth above the 18th green distracted Palmer as he was about to strike the winning putt at the 1960 Masters. Palmer backed away, grinned up at the now-sheepish McKay, readjusted, and sunk the putt. It was the first year "Arnie's Army" buttons began spontaneously popping up on the Augusta grounds after sportswriter Johnny Hendricks dubbed the Fort Gordon soldiers manning the scoreboards and cheering for Palmer as "Arnie's Army." Palmer won $17,500.

APRIL 13

1964

Papers around the country reported on Palmer's fourth Masters victory. *The Augusta Chronicle* wrote, "Arnold Palmer, his jaws clenched in determination until he had it won, broke a lengthy victory drought with a sterling close of 70 to take his fourth Masters Tournament with a 72-hole score of 276, 12 under par."

APRIL 18

1995

Palmer addressed the Wake Forest Heritage and Promise Campaign Convocation after helping it raise $171 million, exceeding its original goal by $21 million. Palmer said, "Friendships brought me to Wake Forest, not the education or the athletics. I didn't learn much Latin or mathematics, but I did learn about myself and about life. I learned more from my professors outside the classroom than I did inside. Every teacher taught me something."

1966

Palmer fended off high winds and Gay Brewer in an 18-hole playoff match to claim the Tournament of Champions title at the Desert Inn Country Club to earn $20,000. He said, "Under the conditions, this was one of my best rounds ever." Brewer, too, was impressed and said, "Arnold played what I think was one of the finest rounds I've ever seen. Yesterday's round was great, but today was unbelievable."

APRIL 23

1969

While playing in the Byron Nelson Classic, Palmer struck what he judged the greatest drive in his entire life. "It went about 400 yards," he said of the tee shot on the 590-yard par-5 3rd hole. "My second shot was a little 3 iron of about 190 yards. So the drive went about 400." He birdied the hole on his way to shooting a 1-under-par 69.

1965

Frank Litsky of *The New York Times* wrote that Palmer has an "animal magnetism" that separates him from other golfers the way Willie Mays had it. "When Palmer is happy, his face lights up," Litsky wrote. "When Palmer is thinking, he frowns. When he plays a bad shot, he scowls, and the world hates the ball for the way it betrayed him."

APRIL 24

1992

While relaxing at Camp David, President George H.W. Bush squeezed in a round of golf with Palmer and Dr. Howdy Giles at Caves Valley near Baltimore.

During practice at the 1996 Masters, Tiger Woods, who considered Arnold Palmer a mentor, and Jack Nicklaus, who considered Palmer a more-than-worthy foe, pose with Palmer. (Howdy Giles)

1967

The *Chicago Sun-Times* reported that two American soldiers serving in Vietnam got more than a free golf lesson after they wrote to Palmer for advice on how to get out of sand traps. "The soldiers received the gear and personal letters from Palmer expressing gratitude for the job they're doing in Vietnam and asking to meet them when they return home," the paper wrote. "Two days later, a package arrived for the men from Palmer containing two sand wedges and 24 golf balls."

APRIL 30
2004

Palmer returned from his 50th appearance at Augusta to the Arnold Palmer Airport and a hero's welcome that made front page news in the *Pittsburgh Post-Gazette*. The newspaper covered the arrival and, after listing his many prestigious accomplishments, wrote. "Then Arnold Palmer did what many say he does best: make people proud to be from Latrobe, Westmoreland County, Pennsylvania. The Greater Latrobe Wildcats high school band plays 'Hot! Hot! Hot!' as he wades into the crowd. Local officials declare it Arnold Palmer Day."

1998

Alexandra Hirn made history by being the smallest baby ever born in The Arnold Palmer Hospital in Orlando, Florida. With the baby weighing just 12 ounces, doctors initiated the birth 13 weeks early to save the life of mother Najwa, who said, "I can't tell you why, but I just knew she would live. She's a fighter."

1961

Palmer won his second consecutive title at the Texas Open at Oak Hills Country Club, earning $4,300.

MAY 6

2006

Gary Player told reporters that golf would be a footnote in Palmer's eventual legacy. "Arnold will be recognized as one of the greatest when it came to giving to society," Player said. "He meant a lot to the world of golf, but what he gave to people every day is more important than what he ever did on the golf course."

1993

Bud Vandiver of Dallas rejoiced that he'd drawn Palmer for the pro-am at the Liberty Mutual Legends of Golf at the Fazio Course at Barton Creek Country Club. "For me, it's a dream come true," he said. "It's a dream come true for every amateur golfer in the world. He is such a gentleman. He *is* golf."

1962

Palmer won the Tournament of Champions at Desert Inn Country Club in Las Vegas to earn $11,000. It was his second consecutive victory.

MAY 7

2006

The *Pittsburgh Tribune-Review* published an editorial cartoon by Randy Bish with the caption: "Cancer researchers at the University of Pittsburgh have discovered the most powerful club ever used by Arnold Palmer." The drawing depicted a golf bag with one big club. The club was labeled, "Generosity."

1990

Golf Digest published a stat that shows Palmer is tops in endorsement money for the previous year. His total take per week from product endorsements, exhibitions, and appearance money was $173,077.

MAY 8

1994

Palmer told reporters he was somewhat skeptical about the idea behind the newly launched Golf Channel until he became exposed to it. "I end up watching it more than I should," he said. "At first, I had some reservations. Finally, I was convinced of the idea of 24 hours of golf."

MAY 9

1964

A powerful group of Texas oilmen invited Palmer to a closed-door meeting. Palmer said: "When I walked in and sat down, they asked me, 'Arnie, if you had our backing, would you consider running for the presidency?' They were dead serious. But it scared the hell out of me. I ran right out of there. In the 1970s, I gave some thought to politics, but Winnie, being practical, said that if I get so upset about one little criticism in a golf story, how in the world am I going to handle politics?"

1962

Palmer and father, Deacon, were caught bantering before a reporter who wrote that Deacon said his greatest athletic achievement may not have been raising a golf legend. It may have happened—not on a golf course—but on a baseball diamond. "I threw a no-hitter once," Deacon said. "It couldn't have been against a bunch of very good hitters," the son said. "They weren't that day," Deacon said dryly.

MAY 30

2006

The first patients were admitted to the Winnie Palmer Hospital for Women & Babies.

1960

Golf Digest recognized a watershed moment in golf: "Apparently, the Arnold Palmer era is under way. No need to look at his 1960 record, either—most golf fans know it by heart. His five wins are almost unbelievable, considering the amount of talent on the tour these days. But when he is going good, he is simply the best there is and unbeatable."

MAY 31

2006

The first baby was born at the Winnie Palmer Hospital for Women & Babies, one day after its opening.

JUNE 2

1993

Jack Nicklaus designated Palmer the honoree for his Memorial Tournament. Nicklaus said, "We've been competitors in almost everything we've ever done. But I'm pleased that through it all we've remained friends. In the early years when I was fighting Arnold, I was really fighting his army. But I never had to fight him. That was very important to me. He never did anything that related to that."

1958

Professional Golfer magazine described Palmer, 29, as "the perfect tournament player. An excellent all-around game, an ideal temperament, and a naturally friendly, crowd-pleasing personality are the trademarks of the new Masters champion."

JUNE 3

1996

Cessna received official certification for its new Citation X, a mid-sized aircraft that immediately became the fastest production business jet. The company announced its plans to deliver its first one to Palmer later that month.

ARNOLD'S ACES

The average golfer is lucky if he or she gets even one ace in their golfing career so Arnold Palmer is by that standard a very lucky golfer. He's had more than one ace. He's had 1.9 of 'em.

And that's not 1.9 aces, that's 1.9 *miles* of aces. That's the total distance if you add up his 20 aces. And no one can be certain if there aren't two, three, or even four more that were unaccounted for. "It's been a problem compiling Arnold's aces," said Doc Giffin, Palmer's personal assistant. "As near as we can figure, he's had 20, but there might be more out there he's forgotten, like the one in Cleveland."

Palmer spent several golf-rich years (1952–54) in Cleveland as a lad stationed there at a Lake Erie U.S. Coast Guard base and later as a paint salesman. The years there were marked by an impatience and ambition to be doing anything but selling paint in Cleveland. He spent every free hour either golfing or dreaming of becoming a great golfer. It was during these years that Palmer completely forgot about a shot most golfers remember until the day they die.

It was 1953 on the 5th hole at Cleveland's Pine Ridge Club. What happened that day was forgotten for 52 years. Then Giffin said he heard from a friend in 2005 who mentioned to him the time he was golfing with Palmer when the then-24-year-old Coast Guardsman/paint salesman knocked in an ace on the 160-yard 5th hole. That well-struck wedge meant the shot wedged itself into the list as Palmer's first out-of-state ace. His first two aces occurred on the dainty downhill 2nd hole at Latrobe Country Club and the third at nearby Greensburg Country Club. Further information regarding specific dates and details are lost to history. Could there have been more in those early years? Maybe. Palmer didn't know for sure.

But even with "just" 20 aces, the facts and coincidences are breathtaking. He's had aces in 11 different states, two countries (No. 14 was March 25, 1988, at the Fuji Electric Grand Slam in Narita, Japan), with every standard club except driver and putter.

Many of his aces are marvels, and that doesn't include the ones that didn't count. He had one on the 238-yard par-3 17th at Bay Hill after a club dispute with an impudent caddie nicknamed TomCat, who had insisted a 3 iron was the right club. Given the distance and the wind, Palmer thought it ought to be a 2, but he relented, went along with his caddies' advice, and wound up leaving the ball short in the drink. Instead of a drop, he grabbed the 2, re-teed, and knocked the mulligan right at the stick. As the ball rolled into the cup for par the really hard way, Palmer shot the caddie an I-told-ya-so glare. But TomCat remained unbowed. "He just stared back at me and said, 'No, sir, you hit that 2 iron fat,'" Palmer said.

In the eyes of golf, that ace was just a workman's par. But he also had three aces in 1965, in March, May, and September. His longest ace drought was 13 years, and that was between No. 9 from September 1966 (a Wilmington, Delaware, exhibition with Jack Nicklaus) to his 10th on September 27, 1979, on the No. 2 hole at Bay Hill's Charger course.

His shortest time between aces? A mere 24 hours. That was September 2–3, 1986, during the Chrysler Cup Pro-Am at the TPC at Avenel in Potomac, Maryland. He aced the 182-yard 3rd hole on consecutive days. Palmer later recalled seeing a TV news crew on the tee the day after the first blast of magic: "I asked what they were doing there filming and they said, 'We're here to film you getting a hole in one.' I told them they were a day late."

Then with a uniquely Palmeresque flare for the dramatic, he repeated the miracle, a feat that was never done before or since in professional golf. *The Washington Post's* Tom Boswell celebrated the sensation thus: "On Tuesday Arnold Palmer made a hole in one. Yesterday he returned and made a hole in a million." Boswell calculated Palmer had played more than 40,000 par-3s and had made "only" 13 aces and figured the odds of him acing the same hole twice in a row exceed 10 million-to-1. By the third day, there were nearly a dozen film crews and thousands of fans ringing the ropes to see if Palmer could possibly pull off a three-peat. I remember asking him if he recalled what he did on the third day. "I don't," he said. "All I remember is it didn't go in. I felt like I'd let a lot of people down."

What might be most remarkable is that 66 percent of the aces—eight of 15—whose dates are verifiable occurred in September with five of those being struck between September 3 through 7.

He celebrated aces on September 6 twice before—once in 1965 in Tennessee and again in 1997 when he aced Latrobe Country Club's 2nd hole for the fourth time. Palmer's last ace was November 8, 2011, at the 165-yard 7th hole on Bay Hill's Charger course with a 5 iron. It was nearly two months after his 82nd birthday.

Even though I literally wrote the book on aces, I'm chagrinned to confess I've never even seen one in person, much less knocked one in myself. Given Palmer's history, my buddies and I often thought it would be fun to unfold lawn chairs on September 6 near the second green at

Latrobe Country Club. Acing on September 6th at Latrobe's 2nd hole would have been a tidy way to tally what may or may not be Arnold Palmer's 21st career ace.

Accomplished athletes who've performed at the highest levels may disagree about which sport is the more difficult, but few dissent on this point: one of the most challenging things to do in any sport is to hit a golf ball with anyone watching. It's because golf is the most self-humiliating game there's ever been. The golf ball is stationary. It doesn't trash talk. Pretty girls have dimples. So do golf balls. For something that doesn't ingest PEDs, the golf ball is incredibly difficult to hit.

So all that means a shot I hit on September 13, 2013, was one of the greatest shots in golf history. Mine, at least. I lipped out a 125-yard pitching wedge with nine people watching. And one of them was, by God, Arnold Palmer. He was sitting with his wife, Kit, in a golf cart on the roadside tee of the 125-yard 2nd hole at Latrobe Country Club. It's a pressure-packed shot to begin with because it's a "beat-the-pro" hole, in which you wager whether you can beat either one of the club's talented assistants. I'd been invited to play at the club's monthly stag event.

As a golf writer, I felt tremendous self-imposed pressure to be good. That's what I was thinking when we began to banter with Palmer and his wife, Kit.

Banter? That part I've got down. I asked if he had any advice on how to ace No. 2, a good question given that he's aced it four times, something I was quick to remind him. "Four times?" he said. "Really? I didn't know that."

This would be off-putting if it were anyone else. Golfers lucky enough to have had aces remember the events with the same clarity as they do the births of their children. I've never had a hole in one, but I remember the four times I've come within inches. I guess he can be forgiven for not remembering his own ace trivia because he's had 20 of them.

Of course, none of this was going through my head as my turn to swing arrived. He's observed me golf before and when he did my only swing thought was: *Just don't crap your pants.* This time I remember thinking, *Ace here in front of Arnold Palmer, and it'll be maybe the coolest thing that's ever happened to you.*

I began to draw the club back. Then right at the crucial moment, I heard: "Honk! Honk! Honk!" Some jackass' car started making noise. Yet I was unfazed. I struck the ball crisply and sent it sailing on a high arc right toward the flag. "Oh, that's going to be good," Palmer gushed.

He was correct. It landed on the fringe, bounced once, and began tracking downhill— middle pin position—right toward the cup. It lipped out! It stopped about 18 inches from glory.

"Nicely done!" Palmer said while giving me a thumbs-up. "And with that horn honking in your backswing. Great concentration!"

I got creamed by my partners, but at the end of the round, all we talked about was what it was like to hit a shot with Palmer watching, and how I did the best. I raced home later to tell my wife all about it. Before I could get started, she interrupted, "Hey, we saw you out golfing! We were pulling out of school, and Josie said, 'There's Daddy! Honk the horn!' Did you hear us?"

JUNE 17

1994

Palmer, the sentimental favorite, missed the cut at the 1994 U.S. Open at Oakmont, but he stirred many in the hometown crowd to tears as he made his final appearance in a U.S. Open. John Mahaffey was Palmer's playing partner. He recalled the final hole, "Arnold has tears in his eyes. It's a fabulous moment, but he has the presence to say, 'Why don't you go ahead and putt first, because yours is more important for you to make the cut. Because when I make it'—and that's how positive Arnold thinks—'these people are going to go crazy.' And he did make that putt." Later in the press tent, Palmer himself was again moved to tears and walked away overcome with emotion by the standing ovation from the news media. Palmer's remarkable day bizarrely competed in the evening newscasts with footage of former commercial sidekick and current murder suspect O.J. Simpson in a white Bronco as he evaded police in a slow speed chase.

1973

Palmer shot a disappointing final round 72 to finish fourth at the U.S. Open at Oakmont. The bitterness of the loss was soothed by the fact that winner Johnny Miller shot a record 63 to stun the golf world.

1966

Palmer's second round 66 tied him with Billy Casper for the U.S. Open lead after round two at Olympic Club in San Francisco. Tied for fifth was Jack Nicklaus, who was angry with USGA officials who had threatened to penalize him for his slow play.

JUNE 18

1993

Shelley Stone, a journalist in Massachusetts, wrote about how she wanted to commemorate her late father's life with an unusual request. She asked Palmer to hit one of her father's golf balls straight into the woods. Palmer wrote back that he fulfilled her request: "The other day I was playing a round of golf at Laurel Valley Golf Club in nearby Ligonier, Pennsylvania. It's a beautiful setting in the foothills of the Allegheny Mountains. I teed up the golf ball and drove it deep into the lush, green woodlands at the edge of the course. It will probably rest there forever. I thought of your father and the nice things you said about him and what he said about me as the ball sailed high over the trees and out of sight."

1974

Palmer's hands were cast in iron and coated in bronze for display in the Dr. Adrian E. Flatt's unusual collection of famous hands on permanent display in the lobby of the George W. Truett Memorial Hospital of Baylor University Medical Center. Palmer's hands joined those of Neil Armstrong; Alan Shepard; Mickey Mantle; eight U.S. presidents, including Abraham Lincoln, and more than 100 other famous men and women in various fields of endeavor.

1962

Newsweek magazine put Palmer on the cover for a story headlined, "How to Put More Steam in Business." The cover caption read, "Arnold Palmer, Perfection Under Pressure." The article speculated on Palmer's chances of winning the Grand Slam and talked about how he combined skill on the course with grace in the conference room where he partnered with Mark McCormack. His daughter,

Peggy, said, "My Daddy really wants to stay home with us, but he can't. If he does, his lawyer will fire him.'"

1960

On the day that Palmer embarked on his most memorable charge to secure perhaps his greatest victory, *The Saturday Evening Post*, one of the most popular magazines in the nation, published a four-page article by Palmer that teased on the cover, "I Want that Grand Slam." In the article Palmer declared that the Bob Jones grand slam of 1930 was no longer possible given the tremendous wealth or job a golfer would need to allow him to dedicate himself to amateur golf. Instead, the new grand slam should be The Masters, the U.S. Open, the British Open, and the PGA Championship. As millions were reading this, Palmer began the fourth round of the 1960 U.S. Open at Cherry Hills 8 strokes behind leader Mike Souchak. In what would become the signature charge of his career, Palmer seized on enormous gallery support and drove the 346-yard 1st hole. Palmer's final round 65 secured him his third major victory, a first-place check of $14,400, and legions of new fans who were wowed by his engaging play and charismatic conduct. Palmer's final line score read 72-71-72-65=280.

JUNE 19

2000

Golfers at Pebble Beach Golf Course began paying $300 greens fees in 2000, money that would help defer the $841 million a group of investors including Palmer, Clint Eastwood, Peter Ueberroth paid to purchase the fabled course (and three others) on the pristine Monterey Peninsula.

1966

Palmer took a 7-stroke lead to the 10th tee of the U.S. Open at Olympic Country Club's Lakeside Course after firing a 32 on the front nine at the Lakeside course. But in one of golf's monumental collapses, Palmer shot a 4-over-par 39 on the back nine while surging Billy Casper's 32 forced a Monday playoff.

JUNE 22

2005

She'd played with Bruce Springsteen; he'd played with Jack Nicklaus, but on this day, Melissa Etheridge and Palmer shared the stage in Philadelphia to offer hope and inspiration to cancer survivors like themselves.

JULY 3

1966

Mike Reasor, Palmer's caddie during the ill-fated collapse at the recent U.S. Open, told reporters that a banned movie camera was distracting Palmer and cost him a crucial bogey that might have altered the ending. "There wouldn't have been any need for a playoff if the Open officials had been on the ball," he said. "Movie cameras were supposed to be banned from the Olympic. But a movie camera in the crowd on the 8th hole cost Palmer a bogey during the third round. It caused him to blast out of a trap 15 feet past the hole. He told me, 'That movie camera is driving me nuts. I can't get set.' But he never officially complained about it."

1936

During this summer six-year-old Palmer began to consistently break 100 at Latrobe Country Club.

JULY 10

1987

On the eve of the 116th British Open, *Golf World* magazine published a Michael McDonnell article about Palmer saying, "It will be a huge injustice if future historians scan the record books and regard the importance of Arnold Palmer as being merely the sum of his championship wins. That's because Palmer's the man who changed the face of golf. He's the one who gave it pace and excitement and lifted it into the realms of high drama whenever he stepped on the tee."

1983

Palmer advocated on behalf of the Senior Tour to the *Hartford Courant*: "The interest of the media and the public is more than anyone dreamed it would be, and if the correspondence I've received from all over the world is any indication, there is no telling how far we can go."

JULY 14

1961

At the height of a fierce gale, Palmer assessed himself a penalty stroke during the second round of the British Open after he struck a wind-nudged ball he believed had come to rest. British golf commentator Leonard Crawley later wrote: "Palmer is a singularly charming young man who plays the game to the letter of the law. When no one else could have possibly seen it, he reported himself as having incurred a penalty on the 16th hole, when the gale was almost at its height and when almost every ball was shivering for mercy."

JULY 16

1988

Gary Player said Palmer should be given a lifetime exemption to play in the U.S. Open and that he would give him his berth if he could. "Yes, if I could give my spot here to Arnold, I certainly would," Player said. "I love golf, but Arnold loves golf twice as much as I do. Arnold Palmer is golf in the United States. He should be here forever."

1987

Playing in his first British Open since 1984, Palmer's putting woes sparked a chagrined comment from outspoken caddie Tip Anderson at Muirfield: "He's a great man, still a wonderful man, but I'm afraid he doesn't putt so well anymore. He missed a couple of 14-inchers, never even hit the hole." Palmer 3-putt four times on his way to shooting 75.

1961

Fresh from winning his British Open championship, Palmer told reporters he had his sights set on the PGA Championship at Olympia Fields Country Club near Chicago. "I want to win worse than ever now," he said. "This could be my year."

JULY 17

1970

As Johnny Carson's stand-in on *The Tonight Show*, Palmer received mixed reviews. Ray Kienzl of *The Pittsburgh Press* wrote: "A Johnny Carson, he wasn't. He flubbed his lines, had trouble reading the idiot board, and cut short conversational subjects to return to the inane script. He probably would have felt more comfortable trying to sink a breaking 4-foot putt for $1 million than sitting in for Johnny

Carson on *The Tonight Show* Friday night. But in his debut as host of a national television talk show, Arnold Palmer handled himself quite well, even if he might have left non-golfers irked by his tendency to talk about a boring subject like golf." Palmer's A-list guests were tennis great Rod Laver and Vice President Spiro Agnew.

JULY 18

1994

Palmer announced he would participate in the 24th annual Greater Erie Charity Golf Classic. Local reporter Kevin Cuneo declared it "great news" for the tournament. "To this day, no other golfer—not Jones, Nicklaus, Hogan, or Snead—comes close to matching the charisma and popularity of Palmer," Cuneo said.

1983

Chattanooga turned back the clock to 1954 to celebrate the unveiling of Palmer's ProGroup Inc.'s new limited edition clubs to commemorate Palmer's pivotal U.S. Amateur victory. The 1954 Arnold Palmer Limited Edition 16-club set sold for $2,650. An optional kangaroo hide bag was an additional $600. Only 3,000 sets of the clubs were offered.

1959

Palmer was asked to speculate about his appeal among the fans. He whimsically suggested, "Maybe it's because I'm in the rough so much that I get to know them personally."

JULY 20

1995

On the eve of his final British Open contest, *USA TODAY* opined on Palmer's work ethic regarding his craft, love for the game, and experience: "It has to be raining hard for several hours for Palmer not to play golf. Considering he has played five or six days a week for 50-some years, he figures he has probably played more rounds of golf than anybody except, maybe, Sam Snead."

1961

Golf-mad pastors seized on Palmer's quote about golf and sermonized how it can be related to life: "You've got to learn to live with trouble and you've got to learn to get out of it."

JULY 21

1995

Palmer, 65, crossed the Swilcan Burn for the last time as a professional competitor. The ovations roared across a town that, as Nick Faldo speculated, would be vastly different had Palmer not first crossed it in 1960. "If there had been no Arnold Palmer in 1960," Faldo said, "who knows, it might have been a little shed on the beach instead of these salubrious surroundings. You cannot say what the man has done for the game. It's everything." *The New York Times* pointed out that the once paltry prize money had exploded into $2 million, that more than 200,000 people paid to watch, and that the merchandise would sell $10 million worth of paraphernalia. The local bank ordered Palmer's name watermarked on the back of each check. Newspapers around the world used words like "spinetingling," "overwhelming," and "breathtaking" to describe the scene as Palmer waved from the bridge and crowds of thousands lining the fairways and hanging from the rooftops cheered themselves hoarse for Palmer.

1970

The Tournament Players Division of the Professional Golfers Association honored Palmer as a thousand of their members converged on the Pittsburgh Hilton to celebrate Palmer's selection as Associated Press Athlete of the Decade.

JULY 25

1988

Shortly after winning the first of two consecutive U.S. Open championships, Curtis Strange told reporters how Palmer took a special interest in him after Strange's father died when he was just 14. "He really went out of his way for me," Strange said. "He never put himself up on a pedestal. He's so human. He makes people feel like he's their best friend."

1971

Palmer won the $250,000 Westchester Golf Classic in Harrison, New York, after storming to a 5-stroke lead over Hale Irwin and Gibby Gilbert. The most lucrative tournament of the year drew one of the best fields with a leader board crowded with top golfers including Sam Snead, Jack Nicklaus, Frank Beard, and Bobby Nichols. It was Palmer's third victory of the year, making it his best year since 1967. Palmer earned $50,000 and a congratulatory call from President Nixon. "He said it was nice for me to lead all the way, and I said it was very thoughtful of him to call," Palmer said. "He told me he wanted to start playing golf again and that when he did he wanted to have a lesson on how to play like I did on No. 16 Saturday when I holed out that bunker shot."

JULY 28

1991

Orlando Sentinel columnist Larry Guest challenged Palmer to quit one or the other: golf or business. He cited the example of amateur golfer Mac Hunter, whom Palmer lost to in the 1946 national amateur championship. Guest asked Palmer if he knew what became of Hunter, "Yes," Palmer replied. "He retired from Riviera C.C. a few years ago and is now lying on the beaches of Hawaii." Guest prodded, "What does that tell you?" To which Palmer shot back, "That tells me he doesn't know about life."

JULY 31
1957

Palmer electrified a future friend and adversary during a practice range warm-up session for the World Golf Championship at Tam O'Shanter Country Club near Chicago. Years later, Gary Player recalled the sensation from the first time he ever saw Palmer swing. "It was the strangest thing I've ever seen," he said. "I saw him take one swing on the practice tee—a drive—and I said this was the best golfer I'd ever seen. One swing. What happened on that swing? That's the first time I ever saw sparks fly when the club hit the ball."

AUGUST 1
1987

Palmer admitted questions about never having won the PGA Championship nag him. "I can remember when I was 37 I really thought I'd win one," he said. "Back then it didn't really bother me. But if enough people keep asking me about it, it does begin to bother you. It isn't going to change my life appreciably that I've never won it. If I won it now, though, it might change my life."

AUGUST 5
1990

During the Paine Webber Invitational, Palmer used a 4 iron to ace the 183-yard 12th hole at the TPC at Piper Glen in Charlotte, North Carolina. It was his 15th career ace.

1989

On the eve of the PGA Championship at Kemper Lakes, reporters told Palmer of Tom Watson's response to a question about never having won a PGA Championship: "Well," Watson said, "Arnold Palmer's never won one either, but I'm still trying." Palmer's reply? "Well, Arnold Palmer's still trying, too!" Palmer's play in the tournament would prove that declaration even more emphatically.

1960

Palmer was asked if his sometimes reckless style of play took a toll on his psyche. "Trouble is bad to get into," he responded, "but fun to get out of."

AUGUST 7

1960

Palmer birdied six of the first 11 holes to wipe out a 5-stroke lead on his way to securing a playoff with Jack Fleck and Bill Collins at the Insurance City Open at the 6,548-yard Wethersfield Country Club near Hartford, Connecticut. Palmer and Fleck continued after they birdied the first playoff hole, where Collins dropped out after a bogey. Palmer then parred the 183-yard 3rd playoff hole and won after Fleck missed a three-and-a-half-foot putt for par. Palmer earned $3,500.

AUGUST 10

1989

Palmer, 59, ignited the galleries and golf fans everywhere by firing five consecutive birdies at the 71st PGA Championship on his way to a 68, just two shots off the opening day lead, at Kemper Lakes in Hawthorn Woods, Illinois. Palmer told the press, "A guy asked me the other day: 'If you didn't know how old you were, how old would you feel?' I told him 29. If I could play and feel like I did today for four days, yes, I could win." He made the cut with a 74, but he shot a disappointing 81 on Saturday. The magic returned for the final round when Palmer shot 70.

1987

Palmer told *Forbes* magazine that he was astounded when he heard Payne Stewart earned $500,000 and that Mike Reid became the first player to top $1 million in career earnings without ever winning a tournament. "Hell, in the 1950s," Palmer said, "you almost had to win or have another job to make sure your family was able to eat."

AUGUST 11

2005

Palmer told reporters he never liked being called "The King." He said, "That nickname is like a lot of nicknames. It's like calling my man, Doc Giffin, Doc. He ain't no more a doctor than I'm a king. Anyway, a lot of people mean it seriously and I'm grateful for that, but no one could be the king of golf. I don't think anybody deserves that moniker."

1989

Newspapers around the country put Palmer's electrifying 68 opening round at the PGA Championship at Kemper Lakes Golf Club in Hawthorn Woods, Illinois, on their front pages. Typical was this Bob Haring report from the *St. Petersburg Times*: "The man who popularized golf like nobody else in history gave his sport another boost Thursday in the only major championship he has yet to claim. Every golf fan should get to watch what Arnold Palmer did during the first round of the PGA Championship. Many of those who did had tears in their eyes. Even Palmer, 59, couldn't help but get caught up in the emotion. 'I've never stopped getting goose bumps,' said Palmer, who had five consecutive birdies en route to a 4-under-par 68, 2 strokes off the lead."

AUGUST 14
2005

Gary Player told reporters that the idea that golf courses needed to be lengthened because today's golfers are stronger was nonsense. "The most shocking statement I heard in a long time," he said, "one of the leading manufacturers of a golf ball said the other day the reason why the ball is going farther is these guys are better athletes than they were in the past. Would you like to see Arnold Palmer arm wrestle Tiger Woods when they were both at their best? Let me tell you, Arnold Palmer would have beaten Tiger Woods."

AUGUST 22
2005

Street & Smith's Sports Business Journal asked CBS golf analyst David Feherty for his dream foursome—living or dead. Feherty said: "I'd play with Arnold Palmer three times."

1993

Organizers for the Bruno's Memorial Classic in Birmingham, Alabama, said Palmer's participation in the tournament had led to a 15 percent surge in ticket sales. Tournament chairman Gene Hallman told a story about how Palmer was responsible for popularizing golf. "A man who'd never heard the history of golf described it as, 'a game invented by Arnold Palmer up in Pennsylvania where you make a long putt on the last hole and win a lot of money,'" Hallman said.

1967

Palmer and Dean Martin hosted the third annual All-American Collegiate Golf Dinner at the Waldorf-Astoria in New York.

AUGUST 24

2004

British national Jane Grey returned home after giving premature birth to her daughter at the Arnold Palmer Hospital for Women and Children in Orlando, Florida, six weeks early. She was so pleased with the treatment she received that she named the child "Millie Palmer."

1954

The unheralded son of a Latrobe, Pennsylvania, greenskeeper began his unlikely quest for the 1954 U.S. Amateur title by defeating veteran New York golfer Frank Strafaci, a seven-time winner of the New York Metropolitan title. Palmer was 1-up in his first of six matches on his march to the title at the Country Club of Detroit. Caddie Jimmy Gill, then 16, remembered the 24-year-old Palmer as businesslike and "great beyond six feet" on the greens "but pretty erratic inside six feet. But he was bold on every putt."

AUGUST 26

1993

Cary Estes of the *Birmingham Post-Herald* wrote, "Arnold Palmer. No other name in sports conjures up such grandiose images of Americana. He is Joe DiMaggio, Joe Montana, and your everyday Joe rolled up into one magnificent, charismatic package. He is simply 'The King.'"

1955

The name "Arnold Palmer" appeared on the top of *Golf World* magazine for the first time as a professional as it announced Palmer's win at the Canadian Open.

SEPTEMBER 1

1986

During the practice at the team-event Chrysler Cup, Palmer fired four shots at the green on the par-3, 182-yard 3rd hole at the TPC at Avenel. None landed on the putting surface. In the next two days, the change in his results at the hole would undergo historic changes.

SEPTEMBER 2

1988

USA TODAY reported that: "Golf course construction is in full swing" and said Palmer Course Design was currently working on 42 projects and had to refuse 12 others because of a full schedule.

1986

Palmer used a 5 iron to record his 12th career ace during the Chrysler Cup Pro-Am at the TPC at Avenel in Potomac, Maryland. Newspapers hailed the "miraculous" shot on the 182-yard 3rd hole. Unbeknownst to Palmer, his miracles on the hole weren't finished.

1971

The Latrobe Country Club, long considered to be "Deke" Palmer's place, now officially became the property of his son as the club announced that Palmer acquired ownership of the place where grew up and learned to golf. Palmer had purchased much of the outstanding stock from Latrobe Steel Co., majority owner.

SEPTEMBER 3

1994

Palmer shot a 75 during the second round of the GTE Northwest Classic at Inglewood Country Club and told reporters that, "golf has been a disaster this year. I haven't played a good round all year. It's tough to balance business with playing. I should probably get on with my business, but it's tough for me to give it up."

1986

Arnold Palmer was surprised to find a camera crew waiting on the 3rd hole at the TPC at Avenel. It was the same hole he'd aced the day before during the Chrysler Cup Pro-Am. Palmer asked why there was such attention. The crew responded, "We're here to film you getting a hole in one." Palmer told them they were a day late then proceeded to use the same 5 iron to again ace the hole, becoming the only professional golfer known to have aced the same hole on consecutive days. Chi Chi Rodriguez joked, "That hole is too easy."

SEPTEMBER 4

1986

Enormous crowds strained at the gallery ropes in the hopes of seeing Arnold Palmer ace the same hole three consecutive days at the 1986 Chrysler Cup Pro-Am. Alas, Palmer's tee shot bounced off the green and into the rough. Nonetheless, the first of several hundred telegrams and letters from well-wishers began arriving at Palmer's Latrobe office congratulating Palmer on the feat of two consecutive holes in one.

1968

Evangelist Dr. Billy Graham made a different sort of pilgrimage as the avid golfer traveled to Latrobe to join Palmer for a round at Latrobe Country Club.

1961

Duffer Richard M. Nixon wound up on the same sports pages that featured headline news about Palmer in 1961. The future president, an 18-handicapper, had aced the 2nd hole at Bel Air Country Club in Los Angeles, calling it the "greatest thrill of my life—even better than being elected." Meanwhile, halfway across the country, Palmer tied for second at Oak Cliff Country Club, host of the Dallas Open, and earned $2,233.

SEPTEMBER 5

1993

Lee Trevino told *Golf World* about Palmer's connection with the fans: "I swear, Arnold would sign an autograph at a red light. If a guy pulled up to Arnold in a car and asked him for an autograph, Arnold would probably pull over if he could read lips."

1963

While visiting Hyannisport, Massachusetts, President John F. Kennedy asked White House photographer Cecil W. Stoughton to film him hitting a golf ball from several different angles with the purpose of showing them to an "interested viewer." Kennedy said he intended to invite Arnold Palmer to the White House to critique his swing sometime later that year following a scheduled trip to Dallas. Kennedy was slain November 22 during that Dallas visit.

SEPTEMBER 6

1988

Golf Digest continued to distribute thousands of "Arnold Palmer for President!" buttons after an August issue included an article suggesting "the only hope for the Republic is for Arnold Palmer to toss his visor into the ring." Sales from the popular buttons benefited the Arnold Palmer Hospital for Women and Children.

1965

Palmer aced the 135-yard 2nd hole at Johnson City Country Club during an exhibition at the Tennessee club with fellow tour pro Doug Sanders. A commemorative *Johnson City Press* article 40 years later noted that Palmer had originally selected an 8 iron, but that J.C.C.C. head pro Theo Abernethy persuaded him that hitting the 9 made more sense.

SEPTEMBER 9

2003

Lanny Wadkins told *The* (London) *Telegraph*: "My generation should get down on its knees for what Palmer has brought to the game—not just in money but the excitement that made golf popular."

1995

Being associated with Palmer meant always being on your best behavior, according to Mark McCormack. He told the *Financial Times* about the day Palmer upbraided him for treating a pestering fan poorly. "He told me judgments are made by things such as what you wear, how you order, and how you treat people in a restaurant. I had been obnoxious to a stupid and arrogant guy at a beach club in Santa Monica. Arnold said to me afterward, 'You have to understand that when you're with me, anything you say is a reflection on me. And I don't treat people like that.'"

1993

A Japanese magazine reported that Palmer still often golfed with former President George H.W. Bush. Palmer said: "We've played quite often since when he was president. He is such a fun golfer to play with. His handicap is 12 to 14. We are close friends, and when he has extra time, we say, 'Let's play.' Usually, one picks up the phone and asks another, 'How about tomorrow?'"

SEPTEMBER 10

2005

PGA Tour commissioner Tim Finchem presented Palmer with a custom-made 1922 steel-wheeled Fordson tractor similar to the one his father drove him around on when he was just three years old. Unlike today's stars, Palmer said it was tractors—not personal trainers—that forged his muscled frame. Power steering was a thing of the future. "I didn't have to lift weights," he said. "I just had to steer that damned old tractor."

1995

Palmer concluded the last round of the GTE Northwest Classic at Inglewood Country Club in California with a stellar 66. It was on his 66th birthday and was noted for being the first time he's ever shot his age.

1989

The 255-bed Arnold Palmer Hospital for Children in Orlando opened to great fanfare. The first baby was born within hours after the ribbon cutting. Within 15 years more than 100,000 children would be born in the Palmer hospital.

1966

Palmer, 37, became agitated by meddling tasks given to him by Winnie in order to distract him from Secret Service men surreptitiously prowling the Latrobe countryside. Unbeknownst to Palmer, they were there to assure the safety of one of the most powerful and popular men in the world who flew to Latrobe for a surprise birthday visit. And for the first time in his life, Palmer's plane was flown without him or his knowledge. Pilot Darrell Brown flew it to Gettysburg to pick up President Dwight Eisenhower for a surprise visit. "I was oblivious to it all," Palmer said, "until I answered the door and found General Eisenhower standing there with an overnight bag. 'Say, you wouldn't have room to put up an old man for the night, would you?' One of the nicest weekends of my life followed. It was the thrill of a lifetime."

1929

Born this day to Milfred Jerome (Deacon) and Doris Palmer was Arnold Daniel Palmer. On this date in 1929, there were fewer than 5,000 golf courses in America, and the sport was considered elitist by the indifferent masses. By 2005 there were more than 16,000 courses, 11,000 of which are public, and major golf tournaments were covered shot-by-shot by top broadcasters.

SEPTEMBER 11

2001

With anxious eyes on newscasts of the attacks in New York, Washington and the plane crash in Shanksville, Pennsylvania, Palmer filmed a promotional video for his new Bay Creek course in Cape Charles, Virginia.

1974

Two days after pardoning Richard M. Nixon, President Gerald Ford flew to Pinehurst, North Carolina, to speak before Palmer and the 12 other members of the charter class at the World Golf Hall of Fame.

SEPTEMBER 12

2005

Palmer, 76, returned to Toronto's Weston Golf & Country Club to commemorate his historic first professional victory at the 1955 Canadian Open and inaugurate the new Kings and Queens Tournament. Preparing to hit the ceremonial first tee shot on the 413-yard 1st hole, Palmer joked, "You know, this hole looks a hell of a lot longer than it did 50 years ago." Still, he boomed two drives down the fairway to earn enthusiastic applause from the gallery. He credited an extensive stretching program with helping him retain his daily vigor. "Throughout my life I've done various things to stay fit—from running to weights to you name it," he said. "Currently, I've been doing something that I've been finding is really very good, and that's stretching. I have a program that I do every day. When I'm traveling I can do it in about 20 minutes. When I'm at home it's a little more extensive. Some mornings it's up to an hour, and I'm very excited about it."

1968

Palmer acquiesced to PGA Tour officials' pleas that he lend his name and prestige to the inaugural Kemper Open at Pleasant Valley Country Club in Sutton, Massachusetts. His first-round 69 generated golf headlines around the country.

SEPTEMBER 13

1993

The magazine, *Senior Golfer*, asked Palmer, 63, if he had any regrets. Palmer said, "I suppose I read too much about Byron Nelson and Bobby Jones and some of the other guys, some of my heroes, who gave up very early in their careers. And maybe I took that too seriously as something that should just happen. Maybe, rather than getting involved in so many other things I should have picked just a couple of things and directed myself at them and continued to play more competitively. But I don't regret it. Those are things I might have changed."

1966

Palmer spent a day at and above Scott Air Force Base in Illinois where he took controls of the C-9 Nightingale and was entertained by General Jack Catton and staff who peppered him with questions about golf as he peppered back with questions about aviation.

SEPTEMBER 15

2003

The 100,000[th] birth was recorded at the Arnold Palmer Hospital for Children.

1984

Palmer, 54, told reporters he'd started wearing a hearing aid: "I never thought I'd do it, but I needed one, so I'm doing it. And you know what? Hitting a golf ball has a whole different sound when you can actually hear it. [It] sounds good!"

1968

Palmer won the inaugural 1968 Kemper Open at Pleasant Valley Country Club in Massachusetts. The $30,000 first-place prize made him the first golfer in history to earn more than $1 million in career earnings. Palmer was only in the tournament after accepting a last-minute plea by PGA officials who'd sought his big name to shore up a field that was attracting sparse attention.

SEPTEMBER 18

1988

Palmer, 59, shot a final-round 70 to win the Crestar Classic at Hermitage Country Club near Richmond, Virginia, and the $48,750 first place prize. It was his 10th win since turning 50. The win, his first in three years, came with frayed nerves. He said, "I never once thought I was home free. When you haven't won in a few years, you always have to wonder if you ever will again."

1974

Palmer, 44, and Broadmoor head professional Duke Matthews beat Anne Sander and JoAnne Carner in a "Battle of the Sexes" exhibition at Broadmoor despite Palmer's atrocious putting. "Will somebody please tell me how to putt?" He pleaded with the gallery. *The Seattle Times* reporter Gil Lyons wrote, "Playing almost flawlessly from tee to green, Palmer holed five birdie putts. His longest birdie was just six feet long. His only long putt was a 15-footer for par." Carner said she started out strong but then "got to watching Arnie, and my game started to slip. He's just so great to watch." Palmer earned $12,500.

SEPTEMBER 19

2005

MacLean's revealed the time NBA great Magic Johnson was introduced to Palmer. Johnson told Palmer how he had built his post-retirement plan entirely on Arnold's model.

1988

Palmer's Latrobe office logged 74 congratulatory calls from fans excited about his Crestar Classic victory.

SEPTEMBER 24

1995

The Westmoreland Museum of Art in Greensburg, Pennsylvania, opened a popular exhibit, "The Art of Winning," featuring 61 of the trophies, cups, belts, and mementoes from Arnold Palmer's golfing career.

1967

Palmer spent an anxious 90 minutes in the clubhouse at Upper Montclair Country Club in Clifton, New Jersey, watching professional football and nervously asking, "What's Nicklaus doing?" When told his lead would hold up and he would win the Thunderbird Classic and its $30,000 first-place paycheck, Palmer said, "You know this is the most money I've ever won in a single tournament."

SEPTEMBER 25

1971

The Wake Forest Sports Hall of Fame inducted Palmer as a member during the halftime of the Demon Deacons' game against Miami, as the Wake Forest band spelled out "ARNIE." Palmer said, "This is undoubtedly one of the finest moments of my life to be here with all of you who have been so great to Arnold Palmer all these years and to accept this honor."

1947

Palmer was immersed in his studies and golf as a freshman at Wake Forest where he earned a golf scholarship. Years later, Palmer confided, "When I was in college, I thought about becoming an attorney, but I wasn't smart enough, I hate being cooped up indoors, and I'm too nice a guy."

OCTOBER 2
1958

A chagrined President Dwight D. Eisenhower wrote Palmer a letter apologizing for failing to recognize The Masters champion during a gala event at Laurel Valley Golf Club near Palmer's Latrobe, Pennsylvania, home. Ike extended belated congratulations and suggested the two play together at Augusta some time but stipulated "judging from the brand of golf I have recently been displaying, I would be more than embarrassed." The letter planted the seeds of what would blossom into a special and historic friendship.

OCTOBER 3
1964

Palmer shared what he expected from a caddie: "Always set the bag down firmly and never hold it by the strap [in case it breaks]; clean the club thoroughly after every shot; be sure the ball is perfectly clean for every putt; always tend the pin for me; if my ball goes in the rough, keep walking in the fairway until you spot it. I don't want you charging in there and accidentally kicking or stepping on the ball and sticking me with a 2-stroke penalty."

OCTOBER 9
1975

Palmer, 45, told reporters he was carrying 183 pounds on his 5'10" frame. "I had a full checkup earlier this year, and the doctors told me my muscle tone was great and that I was in better shape than I'd been in for a while. It took me a long time—about four years—for me to get over the arthritic shoulder condition I developed when I had to pull out of the 1969 PGA after the first round. I went on an exercise program that finally beat the condition in 1970."

OCTOBER 13

2005

Palmer logged his 250th hour in the right seat of his Citation X jet, a position and number significant to pilots in that it allowed the 76-year-old pilot to stay current with FAA regulations. He told reporters: "If my airplane goes, I'm flying either in the left seat or the right seat. And 250 is a lot of hours and a lot of miles when you're flying as fast as we do."

OCTOBER 15

1955

Arnold and Winnie Palmer began settling into the pleasant six-room ranch house built on the slopes across the road from Latrobe Country Club. He paid $600 for the acre and $17,000 cash for the home in which he'd reside through 2006.

OCTOBER 20

1964

In a *Golf Digest* article by Donald Freeman, the author speculated what top golfers might have been—had they not chosen golf. For Palmer he wrote, "Local strong boy. At the carnival all the townspeople urged him to take on the touring Masked Marvel. ['Hundred dollars to any man brave enough to go two minutes with the Masked Marvel!'] He whups the Marvel in two falls. Crowd goes wild!"

NOVEMBER 4

1983

The Golf Course Superintendent's Association of America named Palmer as the recipient of the organization's first "Old Tom" Morris Award for his lifetime commitment to the game of golf and for helping to mold the welfare of the game in a manner and style exemplified by "Old Tom" Morris.

1960

Fresh off a stunning World Series victory against the New York Yankees, Pittsburgh Pirates shortstop Dick Groat celebrated his 30th birthday by enjoying a round of golf with Palmer at Latrobe Country Club. Groat was in the dugout when Pirates second baseman Bill Mazeroski hit the walk-off Game 7 home run that's still remembered as one of the most exciting moments in baseball history.

NOVEMBER 5

1969

Recuperating from hip problems meant Palmer had to set aside the golf clubs, and he admitted that having to go without golf was killing him. "The only way I can get rid of this is rest," he said. "I haven't laid the clubs down for more than two weeks at a time in 10 years. But I've got to do it. Still, whenever I see a golf club, I want to swing it. Stopping smoking is easy compared to this."

NOVEMBER 8

2004

Palmer pilot Pete Luster told *Airport Journals* that flying for Palmer was vastly different from other corporate pilot gigs. "The unique thing about being Arnold Palmer's pilot is that he's always the other pilot. That's significant. When the boss is sitting in the backseat, which is the case for most corporate jobs, you can get away with screwing up. When he's sitting right there beside you, it's pretty tough to do that."

1962

Talk about a tough audience. Palmer had already won 32 times on tour by then, including six major championships, and a reporter asked his father, Deacon, about the state of his son's game. "I believe he finally knows what he's doing on a golf course," he said.

NOVEMBER 16

1962

Veteran British golf writer Keith Marshall said Palmer's July British Open win at Royal Birkdale was due to one club, the 1 iron, and the Harry Vardon low-flying stroke his father taught him. "The winds, which blew during the championship, were of a ferocity guaranteed to separate men from boys. Throughout the tournament Palmer defeated the wind by powering low 1 irons into and below it. I am sure both Palmer's father, who taught his son how to use it, and Vardon, whose name appears six times on the trophy Arnold now holds, would have enjoyed watching those exhilarating 1 iron shots, skimming low like swallows."

NOVEMBER 18

1991

Two generals, Palmer and retired Desert Storm commander General Norman Schwarzkopf, shared a collegial meeting at the Tournament Players Club of Tampa Bay, Florida, at Cheval. Palmer offered to give the hunting and fishing buff some golf lessons. "Then I told him," Palmer said, "when he was ready, we could get our commander-in-chief, President George H.W. Bush, to play with us. He liked that."

1985

Palmer and his three siblings scattered the ashes of their late parents, Deacon and Doris Palmer, on the grounds at Latrobe Country Club.

NOVEMBER 20

1999

In an article titled, "What I Did on My Summer Vacation," Winnie Palmer wrote that, even though she and her husband had been around the world numerous times, "I can honestly count on one hand—leaving several fingers unused—the number of pure vacations we've taken in the past 40 years." She recalled a lovely visit to France and related, "No one in France seems particularly impressed by the sight of a famous American. For me, that's like a dream come true, a chance to relax. But being politely ignored like that can be sheer agony to Arnie, who is used to being noticed and pointed out. To be frank, it makes him uncomfortable when it doesn't."

1966

Palmer sunk what he called "the best putt I've made in 10 years" to save par on the 13th hole on his way to winning the Houston Champions International with a 9-under-par 275. He earned $21,000 and his third victory of the season. His victory over Gardner Dickinson Jr. was wired all over the country by AP and included the line: "When the people root for a millionaire over an average guy, then the money bags man must be something special. Arnold Palmer is."

1962

Look declared the past season as "Golf's Greatest Year." "At a time when more kids, more women, and more seniors are becoming addicted to the game, golf has come up with its greatest troika since the acceptance of the steel shaft. The glamorous trio is composed of Arnold Palmer, Jack Nicklaus, and Gary Player."

NOVEMBER 26
1970

Reflecting on his 1969 Heritage Classic victory, Palmer declared it the most pivotal victory of his career since he won the 1954 U.S. Amateur Championship. "I might come to see it as the most important win of my career," he said. "I wanted it as badly as I ever have The Masters or the Open. It was as hard to win as my first professional tournament...No, it was harder."

1962

The *National Observer* featured a piece on golf through six centuries, and its accompanying timeline included Palmer, "who plays golf the way most people shoot crap. When he swings, it is with all the abandon of a drunk at a driving range."

NOVEMBER 29
1967

When asked about his unflappability, Al Geiberger, winner of the 1966 PGA Championship, said he was a bundle of nerves on one occasion, when he saw Palmer's name behind his on the leader board. "Yeah, I panic," he said. "I was close to breaking up with a bad start in the last round of the 1966 PGA. It was just like when Arnie was behind me in the '65 Classic. When you're leading a tournament and Palmer is only 1 stroke behind you, you know darn well he's there. You have your hands full just trying not to panic."

1959

Arnold Palmer limped to victory with a final round 76 at the West Palm Beach Country Club to win the West Palm Beach Open and $2,000.

DECEMBER 3
1983

Golf magazine listed a compendium of Palmer favorites including: favorite drink, Rolling Rock Light; favorite movies, *True Grit* and *Dirty Harry*; favorite music, Glenn Miller; and favorite golf idol, Deacon Palmer.

DECEMBER 7
1969

Palmer made a vaunted charge with a final-round 7-under-par 65 to win the Danny Thomas-Diplomat Classic and $25,000. Gay Brewer, who led for the first three rounds, said, "As long as I didn't win, I'm glad to see Arnie win it. I really didn't think he had a chance to catch me, although I did respect him." The win gave Palmer back-to-back tour victories, following his surprising Thanksgiving Day win at Harbor Town and erased any doubts that Palmer's previous victory was a fluke. "This thing, this winning, means everything to me," he said. "Getting it going again is probably the thing I wanted most in my life. I knew it was going to happen, that I would play again, but I didn't know how successfully. So far, so good."

DECEMBER 11
1994

Legendary sportswriter Jim Murray wrote that Palmer would always be The King: "He turned golf into a heavyweight fight. Palmer didn't play a course, he slugged with it. Other golfers had failures. Arnold had catastrophes. Anybody can hit a ball off a fairway. Arnold hit 'em off rocks in the Pacific Ocean, out of parking lots, over trees, and through jungles. There was no such thing as an unplayable lie for Palmer. Watching him play golf was like watching Dempsey fight, Kelly dance, or Mays go after a fly ball. It wasn't that he had a gorgeous swing—he slashed at the ball like a guy beating a carpet."

DECEMBER 13
1988

Palmer told reporters his engaging on-course personality came from trying to deal with a temper that nearly got him banned from golf: "Dad threatened me with having to give up golf if I couldn't control my temper. The way I did it was by talking to people and making conversation out of a bad shot."

1962

The *Rand Daily Mail* hailed Palmer's appearance at the Transvaal Open as unprecedented in South African golf history. Palmer "makes this provincial tournament the most exciting on this year's South African circuit—if not in South African golfing history. There is promise of rich drama and low scoring—by those who keep on line, but for those whose tee shots find the rough, the penalties promise to be heavy." The article noted Palmer had three-putted just once in five matches against hometown favorite Gary Player.

DECEMBER 14
1989

Veteran sportswriter Thomas Boswell of *The Washington Post* answered the question, "What's He Really Like?" about the top golfers he'd covered for the past 15 years. Of Palmer he wrote, "The man's blessed with the gift of naturalness. Always seems at home in his own skin: relaxed, generous, forceful, almost no vanity, has the knack of seeming tired, slightly irritated, yet forbearing—a great man enduring his greatness. Likes people. Remembers names. Still mischievous. Even more handsome in person—in a grizzled, Clint Eastwood way—than he looks on TV."

DECEMBER 15

1994

Payne Stewart told reporters about the first time he played a round with Palmer. "It was in the L.A. Open at Rancho Park," he said. "I was in the second-to-last group with Arnie and Lanny Wadkins. This was back in 1983, so I'm a pretty young guy on the tour. I remember the galleries were lining both sides, and it's 'Go Arnie!' and 'Sign my tractor. I use Pennzoil!'…On one hole I hit one inside 10 feet, and it's polite applause. Then Arnie hits it to about 40 feet, and it's a huge roar, 'Yay, Arnie!' Another hole, I hit one through the green, and the gallery hardly moves. I mean, they leave me hardly any alley to hit through. I go back there, and my first chip hits the edge of some lady's chair. I'm steaming. My next shot, I chip in, and some guy applauds and says, 'Nice shot.' I got a very important lesson in my golf career that day. I learned if I wanted the galleries to support me, I'd have to learn to behave like Arnold Palmer."

DECEMBER 20

1969

While at a gala White House Christmas dinner, President Richard M. Nixon called on Palmer to make some extemporaneous remarks. Palmer took the opportunity to needle Nixon about inserting himself into the debate over who ought to be the No. 1 college team in the nation. Nixon had asserted it ought to be the Texas Longhorns, while Pennsylvania partisans, including Palmer, thought unbeaten Penn State ought to be ranked first. "I'm honored to be speaking before such a great football expert," Palmer joked.

1968

Palmer sportswear was now available in more than 4,000 stores. Sam Connell of Loveman's department store in Birmingham, Alabama, said, "In my estimation, Palmer is the name people know, the name they ask for, the name they buy. Therefore, we concentrate on Palmer. We go with the champion all the way."

1956

For the first time, the name Palmer appeared on the top 20 leading money winners list. He earned $16,144 to finish 19th.

1954

Palmer, 25, and Winifred Walzer, 19, ran away to elope in the Falls Church (Virginia) Presbyterian Church before a small circle of Palmer family and friends and no Walzers. Palmer's future father-in-law, Shube Walzer, boycotted because he was convinced his daughter was making a tragic mistake.

DECEMBER 21

1964

Chi Chi Rodriguez was asked if any fellow pros had ever objected to his crowd-pleasing antics. "Just one," he said. "Arnold Palmer. He told me my behavior was bothering him. Well, the day he said it was bothering him was at The Masters, and he'd just shot a 68. Oh, how I would like to be bothered like that!"

1957

Palmer finished fifth on the money winners list with $27,802, an $11,000 jump over his previous year's earnings.

DECEMBER 24

1969

Local newspapers reported Palmer stopped by the Youngstown, Pennsylvania, Fire Department to have a holiday drink and laugh with his neighbors as Christmas neared.

1966

Reacting to the news that Billy Casper was the PGA Player of the Year, *The Sporting News* wrote: "If it seems a paradox to refer to Palmer as the king of golf and then to Casper as the Player of the Year, it's because it is indeed a paradox. Palmer is still the king, the general of the army. Since his collapse at the Open, Palmer has come on strong and is again flashing the form that carried him to the summit."

DECEMBER 27

1970

Famed New York restauranteur Toots Shor submitted his application for membership at Palmer's new Bay Hill Club & Lodge. Included were the requisite $250 check and the following references: "President Richard M. Nixon, Vice President Spiro Agnew, and Arnold Palmer."

DECEMBER 28

1975

Lee Trevino told reporters that the reaction to him, Jack Nicklaus, or Fuzzy Zoeller standing individually was always the same: polite applause. "But Arnold stands on the tee, and they go crazy. They yell and clap and stamp their feet. It's charisma. He has it. He has more than anyone's ever had, probably more than anyone ever will."

DECEMBER 30
1972

The *Pittsburgh Post-Gazette* printed a front page article based on a wire Palmer wrote to Chuck Noll as the coach's Pittsburgh Steelers were making a run to the Super Bowl behind running back Franco Harris. It read: "I'm ordering my army to join ranks with Franco's and all your other support forces for an all-out assault on the Miami Dolphins on Sunday. How appropriate that all of this started in July at your summer camp here in Latrobe, the real cradle of pro football. Regards, Arnold Palmer, On to L.A.!"

DECEMBER 31
1973

Palmer, who became the first member of the PGA's million dollar club in 1968, topped the year by becoming—along with Jack Nicklaus—the only player to have grossed $2 million in total earnings (winnings and sponsorships).

1964

Looking back on the year that was, *Golf* magazine said it was a bad year for golf widows, and it was bound to get worse: "Now, even when her hero has been snowed off his favorite course, he can still spend four or five hours each weekend watching the game's top professionals perform on television. Television golf has grown to the point where Arnold Palmer has become as much a show business personality as Jackie Gleason, Ricky Nelson, or Efrem Zimbalist Jr."

1955

Palmer's first pro season ended after 31 events. He missed the cut six times, his scoring average was 70.99, and he earned $8,226.

Chapter 14

Palmer's Final Days

I saw Arnold Palmer twice in the six months before he died. The first time an infected foot left him hobbling along on a walker, and recent oral surgery—he was down to eight of his orginal teeth—left him slurring his words through a gummy grin. Every step looked like a grim torture.

With six months to live, Arnold Palmer looked like a man with six months to live.

It was May 28, 2016. A golf writer friend of mine, Jason Deegan of Golf Channel, was in western Pennsylvania to write a travel preview for anyone who'd be coming to Pittsburgh to enjoy the U.S. Open at Oakmont. So we toured the club, the course, and the office. My ground rules always included the admonition that if he was even there we were not to bother Mr. Palmer. We could tour the building, but it was unlikely—in theory—we'd get to meet the man.

In practice it was always the exact opposite. If you were in the building, he'd want to meet you. That's how it was with Jason. Palmer, a man who looked like he belonged in an intensive care bed, rose to greet us. He couldn't talk, but he gingerly removed his right hand from the walker and gave us that famous thumbs-up.

I really admired it. Because of innate human vanity, had most of us been in that condition, we'd be sequestered in some dark room refusing all visitors. Not him. He knew the world was full of people who wanted to say, "Hey, I met Arnold Palmer." And for as long as he could remain upright, he was not going to disappoint them.

His appearance shocked my friend. Deegan said, "He looked incredibly pale and frail. He could barely stand, and his handshake was practically limp. News that he'd been in decline had leaked out, but I think the general public had no idea just how rapidly he'd declined."

Then we stood there and watched as he, incredibly, was helped into the driver's side of a waiting golf cart and zoomed down the driveway. Was he going to his house? To the club? To the cockpit? Even on a walker, he remained utterly untamed. I was told later he'd already nearly killed himself driving into the building, into parked cars, and off steep hills, but there was nothing they could do. Palmer was going to do as he damn well pleased.

Later at The Tin Lizzy, Jason and I recounted the exhilarating encounter and morosely speculated he'd never make it six months. Heck, if he still had unfettered access to that golf cart, he might be done by dinner. He couldn't talk or walk. Neither of us could have predicted that day how Palmer had one more charge to the finish.

Because on August 7, *Kingdom Magazine* surprised me with an assignment: could I interview Arnold Palmer for a Q&A the next week? I explained how the Q was a cinch, but I didn't know about the A. It seemed a preposterous imposition on a sick old man. A lot of people had been wondering about The King's health. His office turned down a deluge of interview requests in June when the U.S. Open was held at nearby Oakmont. I'd seen with my own eyes just how diminished he'd become. But my editors had been assured he'd be up to it.

Indeed, he was. It was an hour I'll forever treasure. I wouldn't say he'd found the fountain of youth, but it was more like he'd sipped from the fountain of stability. Gone was the walker, the stumbles, and slurs. He was his old self. Still old, but once again himself. He shook my hand warmly and immediately disarmed me by saying: "Chris, how've you been? I've missed you! What are you going to try and stump me with today?"

The restoration of the twinkle in his eye nearly put a tear in mine. After seeing him so near death, his revival had me feeling truly ebullient. It was remarkable. I don't know why I should have been surprised. He'd been left for dead many times over the years but came roaring back on the final nine to win 92 championships. I asked if he'd been behaving like a good patient. "Some days I am, and some days I'm not," he said. "The tough thing about being under a doctor's care is just doing what they tell you to do. That was my problem today. I was having a little trouble keeping my balance, but they help me a lot, and I like them."

A bottle of premium bourbon was on his desk. I asked if it was medicinal. He said, "Oh, someone gave me that and told me it was a cure for all." He winked when he told me some smiling lies about his plans to hit balls later that day. He said this all the time. I think he knew people around the world would feel better about life if they knew somewhere back in Latrobe, Pennsylvania, Palmer was taking divots in a restless quest for striking the perfect shot.

In fact, he'd rarely swung a club since December 2014 when he fell and dislocated his shoulder on his way to dinner at the PNC Father-Son Challenge at the Ritz-Carlton Golf Club in Orlando, Florida. I asked if he'd ever felt like giving up. (We were talking about golf, but his answer nimbly applies to life.) "I've had that feeling, sure," he said. "I've felt my game would let me down a little, but it always came back, thank goodness. I think the reason it did is because I never truly lost confidence. I never ever thought it was over."

I asked if he enjoyed sitting for hours while famous artists like Norman Rockwell or Leroy Neiman painted his portrait. He said some complimentary things about the artists before adding, "Honestly, I'd rather be golfing."

And as my very last question, I asked him a personal one. Will there be golf in heaven?

Editors chose to not use the question or his answer in the edition that hosted this session. I supposed they were ghoulishly planning on using it for commemorative issues after he'd died, which is precisely what they did. Anyhow, here is what he said: "Oh, I think there will be a lot of golf in heaven. I'll bet Nelson and Hogan are up there having a match right now. I know a lot of guys who've been good golfers who are looking forward to resuming great matches with friends and family just like they did here on earth. I think the courses will be a lot like the ones here. But the hazards will include clouds that get in the way of approach shots."

In fact, my last question to Palmer was the same as one of my first. When I was doing that old hole-in-one book and asking him about aces at Laurel Valley, I was pitching a story about what golfers and clergy felt about the divine possibilities. And I'd asked him about it again on and off over nearly 15 years of interviews. I never found an editor interested enough to pursue it, even though it always electrified Palmer, a man who'd seen plenty of heaven on earth. His eyes would light up at the question, and his answer never deviated. He'd clearly given it a lot of thought. Affirmative. He said there would be golf in heaven. What would heaven be without golf?

I didn't know it would be the last time I'd see him. In fact, I left the office and immediately called my friend Jason and told him of Palmer's miraculous recovery. "He looks," I said, "like he could go another two years. He's just amazing."

He'd be gone in 39 days.

Because much has been made about how much he loved golf and how much he loved aviation, those were always the mere surface topics whenever we sat down to talk. And they obscure one true love at the heart of our every exchange. Palmer loved life.

Had I known then it would be the last time I'd ever see him, I'd have dropped my pen and thrown my arms around his once-robust, now-tottering frame and told him how much I loved him. I'd have thanked him for his friendship.

Who's to say if there's golf in heaven? All I know is heaven became more heavenly the instant Palmer started calling heaven home.

On September 25, 2016, Arnold Palmer died at 6:03 PM in UPMC Shadyside hospital in Pittsburgh. He was taken to an operating room where surgeons were preparing a complicated procedure intended to address the problems that ultimately killed him. He suffered a massive heart attack. Doctors said he died instantly. The official cause of death is asystolic arrest.

He'd spent the previous two nights at nearby UMPC Presbyterian where he arrived by private helicopter flown by longtime friend Ed Kilkeary of LJ Aviation. Despite his evident infirmities, Palmer insisted on riding in the front seat.

Kit Palmer, his second wife, and Palmer's daughters, Peggy and Amy, had all been at the hospital. Kit right away called his best friend, Doc Giffin. His official title since 1966 was simply "assistant." Palmer had said in a 2015 *Golf Digest* profile that Giffin's "real title ought to be 'friend' or 'everlasting friend.'"

The heartfelt compliment on that Sunday evening became freighted with added poignancy. "The world lost an icon, but I lost my best friend," Giffin told me. "I was stunned and, of course, saddened. We knew the surgery was to be serious but had to be done. It was shocking, though, that he never got to the operating room, but it wasn't totally unexpected."

Giffin had indeed been blindsided. Two hours before the news of Palmer's passing broke, he and I engaged in one of our long, chatty email exchanges about the cast of *Survivor: Millennials vs. Gen X*. If Doc had suspected Palmer was in any jeopardy, he wouldn't have been frittering away the afternoon about trivial matters like Jeff Probst and his reality game show contestants.

Giffin said he was saddened by having to observe this once-robust man slowly decline to "almost an invalid in the end." Still, Palmer died the way the golfing great had hoped he would.

"His father died of a massive heart attack, and the doctors said he died instantly," Giffin said. "In the days after that, Arnold told me he hoped that, when it was his time to go, he'd go the same way. His doctors tell me that's exactly what happened."

I'm touched by the number of people who've reached out to me over the death of a man I was privileged to call a friend. They said it's going to be alright, that time heals all wounds, and that he's gone on to a better place.

Arnold Palmer, the drink, is one part lemonade, three parts unsweetened ice tea. Arnold Palmer, the person? To me, he was one part champagne, three parts beer. In that way, he was much like his hometown. And all of the parts of Latrobe were about to begin to mourn.

The first sign appeared in town the very next morning. Fittingly, it appeared at a place renown for vision. It was the sign outside The Eyeglass Shoppe on U.S. Route 30. In bold letters it said, "Thank You

Arnold Palmer. You Will Be Greatly Missed." Allen Jurica used to take reading glasses frames over to the office for Palmer to pick his favorites. "I just wanted to make a small gesture to let people know we were thinking of him," Jurica said. "In a town this size, everyone has some connection to Arnold Palmer and to one another. It's just the way it is."

Others soon followed suit. Signs that usually advertised beer and wing specials at Sharky's and down the highway at Dino's, popular competing sports bars, changed their signs to Palmer tributes. It happened with dry cleaners, bakers, beer distributors, and even fast food joints in defiance of corporate conformity policy. Understand, these businesses were not only honoring an icon, but also a customer. A favored son was being thanked for a lifetime of favors. Latrobe was tentatively beginning to grieve. This had to be done proper before it felt at ease to celebrate. And celebrate, by God, it did.

Grieving the loss of a loved one can be very personal. It might mean stealing a reflective moment at a place of solitude or kneeling in a place of worship. The death of Palmer was wholly communal, and many of us consecrated together in local taverns. It was like that all week at The Tin Lizzy. Organizers for the elaborate memorial at St. Vincent Basilica built in a nine-day lag to accommodate the professional golf world as it participated in the Ryder Cup in Chaska, Minnesota, and the busy schedules of various dignitaries. The out-of-towners filled up the Palmer Marriott, the nearby Wingate, and all the cozy guest homes at the club. Many of them were eager to experience the charms of Latrobe. Sooner or later, many of them found their way to The Tin Lizzy. The building dates back to the '50s—the 1750s.

It has a basement Rathskeller. This is where the bones of the old Tin Lizzy rattle loudest. Low timber rafters and bedrock fireplaces give warm ambiance, and the actual bar is about 50 feet of one-piece solid timber. It's all gnarly and varnished. Longtime owner Buck Pawlosky talks about the day he and a squad of hearty friends took out a window and spent the day painstakingly maneuvering the novel bar top into place. The "new" part of the building—everything above the basement—was built in the 1890s. The ground-level main bar with its sparkling picture window on one side. On the other side is a rattling old wheel of fortune that lets customers spin for free drinks or—hooray—a can of free Spam! It's the kind of place where in the summer someone's always leaving a basket full of surplus garden vegetables, and in the winter, they're right there ready with jumper cables for when you're in a frozen fix.

The dining room behind the bar seats 36. The second floor bar and outdoor deck is Flappers, a 1920s-themed bar so elegantly appointed that local advertisers use it to film commercials. It's a martini bar tucked so discretely back into the building that wandering into it feels like discovering a secret speakeasy. And the Tin's third floor has been my office—my actual office—since 2015. Prior to that my office had been from 2007 above another landmark Latrobe bar, The Pond. Renovations there meant a move here.

Palmer and Kit came in for dinner every other week or so. They'd eat in the dining room. Kit is said to be enamored with the Rathskeller. Her husband seemed most at home in the Main Bar. Bartender Jim Sciabica kept a special bottle of Palmer's requested PM Whiskey tucked away behind the bar. It's still there untouched since Palmer's last shot. It's Jimmy's personal tribute to the memory of a man he so admired. "He was just this great guy," he said. "At heart he was always just working class, just like the people who hang out here. This was his kind of place."

And his old man's. In fact, Palmer is a second generation regular. In his 2000 autobiography, *A Golfer's Life*, Palmer wrote about his father's enduring affinity for the landmark hotel when it was Amer's. "He loved drinking shots and beers with his buddies at the firehall or at Amer's Hotel in Youngstown," Palmer said.

How much did Palmer love The Tin Lizzy? He offered to buy the whole shebang from Pawlosky. Buck had owned it since 1980. "Yeah, it was one of those nights when everyone was having a great time," Buck said. "He came up to me with a big smile on his face and said, 'I'd like to buy your bar.' He told me to call his office the next day. I did, but they just laughed and said he must have been feeling overcome by the moment."

Given the history of the building and Palmer's affinity for the landmark, it's understandable some wild rumors have sprung up about Palmer and the Tin. It's been said he lived here (false), that he was born here (false), and that his father lived here (true). All we know for sure was he was very happy here and that he loved the place and the people. It was one of his hometown haunts.

I was thinking of this the Friday before the memorial. He'd been dead just five days. Somber moments remained, but I remember thinking how it was starting to feel like a party, a celebration. Earlier that day there'd been the private family funeral, the solemn spreading of his ashes at the club, but it was not before one last ceremonial flight with his remains.

It was that flight that launched the Palmer rainbow phenomenon. A light rain had been misting Latrobe that afternoon. The instant Palmer's ashes began their ascent, the clouds parted, and a vivid rainbow appeared. The Palmer rainbow appearing to spread across the Palmer Regional Airport from Latrobe to the country club went viral and even made the network news.

It would be the first of three. Another appeared during the memorial, and a third materialized at the June 25 Westmoreland County Airshow held in tribute to Palmer.

I had the first day's rainbow on my mind that evening when I popped in for a double Jack Daniel's on the rocks (no straw) at Flappers. The bar was empty, but on the porch, there were about a dozen people who were loud and raucous. I asked the bartender what was going on. "Oh, they're telling all their Arnold Palmer stories," she said. "They've been out there for two hours. I don't think they're ever going to leave." I stayed for about 30 minutes, and it was like you could have set your watch. A roar of laughter took place every 90 seconds. I thought someone was going to call the cops. I closed my eyes and imagined Palmer was at the table with all his neighbors and reveling in all the hometown fun.

Another Tin Lizzy rumor, and this one has some legs, is that the creaky old place is haunted. Some have said they've heard sneezes in empty rooms, heard footsteps dragging on crooked hallways, and everyone remembers the dark night the new Flappers bartender fled the building—never to return—after screaming she'd seen the grinning young girl in the red dress.

When I wrote this chapter, it was near midnight, and The Tin Lizzy was empty. I was all alone. The remnant gusts of the latest devastating hurricane were lashing western Pennsylvania. The winds whistled through age-warped frames, and the old building creaked and moaned like an arthritic skeleton trying to get up and stumble away. In four minutes the calendar would turn, and it would be a new day. Coincidentally, it would be September 25, 2017, one year to the day when Palmer left us.

★★★★

The skies were clear above the Arnold Palmer Regional Airport on October 4, 2016, but they were crowded. One after another, the private jets kept coming in low over Rusbosin Furniture to touch down on the runway. It was like watching a well-organized migration of some of the wealthiest and most influential people in America.

They came from Europe and all over the United States to pay homage to a man who simultaneously rose to iconic heights from humble origins but never once dreamed of abandoning them. The 60 private jets momentarily made the airport tarmac look like a used car lot if all the jalopies were $23 million high-tech aviation marvels.

They were organized and safeguarded by Gabe Monzo and his stellar crew of staffers, and ground personnel. He knew these cool professionals could have handled the influx with skilled ease, but something told him he belonged with them on this special day. So Gabe skipped his friend's memorial.

Famous attendees included Ernie Els, Tom Watson, Annika Sorenstam, Lee Trevino, Phil Mickelson, Nick Faldo, Tom Ridge, and Rickie Fowler to name just a few. Darius Rucker was there, too. CEOs and associates from more than three dozen Fortune 500 companies stopped what they were doing to be there. I had speculated at least two presidents of the four living ex-presidents would attend—and one of the candidates wanted to be there—but all were discouraged lest any of them during that heated 2016 presidential election season made the ceremony appear at all political.

Davis Love III was the last to arrive. Frazzled over the possibility of being late for something special, he asked the quickest way to get to St. Vincent Basilica. Monzo pointed to his vehicle and said, "Jump into that Suburban right there and just hang on."

They made it with time to spare.

More than 1,000 people packed the basilica that day; another 5,000 watched via closed circuit at various locations around the campus. And this being St. Vincent, the summer home of the Pittsburgh Steelers, some fans arrived early and hosted tailgates.

So much of the day seemed so surreal, like a dream. My wife, a buddy of ours, and I got there 90 minutes before the start of the 11:00 AM ceremony. In some regards we arrived late. We barely got a seat clear in the back. The pews were packed with golf royalty. We sat right next to Bob Goalby. He won The Masters in 1968 after Roberto De Vicenzo famously made a scoring error and was disqualified after innocently attesting to the mistake by signing the scorecard. The incident is still recalled any time the haughty precision of the rules of golf are debated.

Seated in front of us and rocking a neon blonde punk buzzcut was a friendly Connellsville woman who said she was Palmer's twice-a-week masseuse. What did Palmer say to her? "He asked if he thought he'd look good with a haircut like mine," she said. Professional ethics, she said, prevented her from dishing any further intimacies.

The speakers were almost all funny or moving—especially Jim Nantz—in sharing their Palmer stories. If you see Nantz and want to make a good impression, compliment his speech at the Palmer memorial. The recollection will exhilarate him. He may have looked composed, but he admitted to me nearly a year later he was a bundle of nerves. "It was one of the hardest things I've ever had to do," he said. "I was more nervous about doing well for that than I was for any assignment—and I've broadcast seven Super Bowls." He truly rose to the occasion. He was funny, poignant, and insightful—the immaculate picture of warm composure.

Palmer grandson Sam Saunders told a great story about how his grandfather never let anything come between him and his loved ones. He said he called and asked Palmer what he was doing. Palmer said he was talking with the president. Saunders asked, "The president of what?"

"Of the United States," Palmer responded.

Saunders asked why he took his call when he was standing in the Oval Office. "I wanted to talk to you," Palmer said.

Vince Gill was pitch perfect in his every utterance, but I've never seen him when he was anything but. After Jack Nicklaus told a story about how a then-stoic Palmer had admitted to tuning out his hearing aids the day he was honored in Washington, D.C. with the Congressional Medal of Freedom. Gill performed at that D.C. ceremony and deadpanned, "He said I was his favorite singer. Now I know he never heard me sing a note." Gill, who had been coming to visit Palmer for years and is the runaway celebrity crush of the sweethearts who worked in Palmer's office, said Palmer was his favorite person. "Not my favorite golfer," he said, "my favorite person."

Tom Ridge, a man who's been involved in the sacred memorials of many fine men and women, told me it was the most magnificent memorial he's ever attended. "I've never been to a memorial service that so eloquently captured the spirit of a human being so worthy of universal emulation," he said. "Everyone should make sure they watch the video of that entire memorial. It should be taught in schools."

Chapter 15

Latrobe's Legacy

John Garvey drove halfway across country to visit Latrobe, Pennsylvania, knowing that, barring the supernatural, there was zero chance he'd get to meet Arnold Palmer. It used to be a given you'd see him. Palmer was everywhere. You'd see him in restaurants, at library fund-raisers, at newsstands, at barber shops, at grocery store lottery ticket counters, and most definitely at the country club. Even in his twilight years, you'd see him patrolling the course, forever eager to offer gentle encouragement or maybe make a brand new friend.

Garvey felt compelled to be here, and, while Palmer was gone, the spirit of Palmer was transcendent. "It was like he was right there with me the whole time," he said. "Every aspect of my visit felt especially spiritual to me in that way. I made so many new friends."

Days after the memorial's conclusion, Garvey visited Latrobe, Pennsylvania, traveling all the way from his home in Oklahoma City. That's where Garvey has lived all his life and where the attorney took the day off from to watch the Palmer memorial. He'd tried to convince friends to go, but the mission was one-by-one rejected as senseless.

Dakota Murley probably wishes at least one of them would have agreed and sparred him some anxious embarrassment. Murley was the longtime boyfriend of his daughter Samantha. So Garvey, a Palmer fan since he was seven, was fully immersed in his viewing and admittedly becoming emotional. "I was fine," he said, "right up 'til Nantz took the podium."

That's right about when Murley entered the room with a respectful request to speak. Through tear-rimmed eyes, Garvey looked at the young man and said, "I'm not doing anything until this is over. Is there something you need from me?"

"I'm here," he said, "to [gulp] ask how you feel about me marrying your daughter."

"I reached for the remote and hit the mute button and said, 'Son, you and I are gonna have a conversation about this, but that's not going to happen until this is over,'" Garvey said.

Fear not, romantics, hours later Garvey gave his ascent, and on October 21, 2017, Dakota and Samantha Garvey became husband and wife. And, oh, how Palmer would have loved that story.

John Garvey's is another kind of love story, one you may share. He loved Palmer. Garvey said he felt so grief-stricken when he heard Palmer died that he acted on his compulsion that he had to visit Latrobe to pay tribute to Palmer.

He has a passion for sports cars, and daughter Samantha knew to keep an eye out for "unicorns," exceedingly rare models. And she found one in New Jersey just days after her father had wept while viewing the memorial. It was a 2004 Ford SVT Cobra painted competition orange. Garvey has a thing for orange, and there were only 72 made. He had to have it, sure, for the car but also for the role it could play on his quest. And the car was secondary to the quest. The 1,500-mile trip would take a full day. But Google Maps showed a convenient route that rolled nearly right through Latrobe.

Gentleman, start your engines.

He pulled the shiny orange Ford into the crowded parking lot at the Palmer SpringHill Suites Marriott. It exceeded his expectations. "It's like a museum unto itself," he said. "The thing I remember was walking in and seeing this shiny object across the lobby. It was a Masters trophy. It had one of his golf bags, a cardigan sweater, and dozens of pictures and exhibits."

But did it have a room? "The desk clerk said, 'You're in luck, sir. You can have our last one.' It went like that the next 72 hours. I was lucky the whole time." The clerk told him about the time in 2012 when Palmer asked her to come with him to chaperone then-presidential nominee Mitt Romney from the airport to the hotel during a campaign stopover.

Any visitor to Latrobe, Pennsylvania, should stop at The Tin Lizzy. Arnold Palmer used to frequent the bar, and the building dates back to the 1750s. (Chris Rodell)

HOTELS AND BOOKS

You have to secure a gritty job with boiler room access to see my second favorite Arnold Palmer autograph. It would likely entail a drastic career change, but it's worth it. First consider the artistry of the Palmer pen. Plastic surgeons are less careful suturing scars on supermodels than Palmer was when signing an autograph. He appreciated that many of his signed artifacts would be framed and mounted in conspicuous places for multitudes to admire.

But a concrete example—literally—of just how meticulous he can be with his signature is visible to just a handful of maintenance workers who venture into a room few even know exists. It's the sprinkler room in the bowels of the $8.5 million SpringHill Suites by Marriott. It opened in November 2012 on Arnold Palmer Drive about a half mile from Latrobe Country Club. The nearly two-foot long signature isn't as precise as more conventional signings, but no one can argue he was rushed.

It took him an hour to complete the signature and, like the final round drive on No. 1 at the 1960 U.S. Open at Cherry Hills, the man really nailed it. Brad Thomas was the hotel's senior project manager. He saw the whole thing and discussed it on the hotel roof during a pre-opening tour in July 2012. "He climbed down in a hole, so the floor was about waist high. He took a two-inch nail and scratched his name in the wet concrete," Thomas said. "He was unhappy with how it looked so he grabbed a trowel and erased it. He came back an hour later when the concrete was a little more set. It's beautiful and will be there long after me and the men who built the building are gone."

Thomas, the hotel builder, is a man of many hats, and most of them are hard. Besides shepherding multi-million dollar construction projects coast-to-coast, he's owned saloons near Nashville (Losers Last Chance II), and raced quarter horses in Colorado. And he's just a lot of fun. Watching him interact with the crew must have been like watching General George S. Patton preparing his troops for battle. He is fluent in profanity, suffers no fools, and talked about the man he called "The Big A" the way schoolgirls do when they think they're in love. "I've worked construction for owners all across the country, and most of them look at guys like me like we're tools, not people," he said. "Not him. Hell, if that man asked me to build him a Taco Bell in Nova Scotia in winter, I'd start packing my parka. I never thought I'd meet a man I could admire as much as I admire my own father, but The Big A came close. We took a lot of pride in building this place because we knew we were doing it for him. And he's not a man anyone would ever want to disappoint."

The hotel is a Marriott in name only. The place is pure Palmer. Each of the three lodging floors was themed to remind guests of marquee courses pivotal to the Palmer legend (Augusta National, Oakmont, and St. Andrews are the honorees). "The place is like an Arnold Palmer museum," said John Beckwith, who has stayed there during his annual visits to golf and while attending Pittsburgh Steelers training camp at St. Vincent. "And you never know who you're going to meet at the bar when the Steelers are in town. Be there one hour, and it's pretty much guaranteed someone is going to let you try on their Super Bowl ring." Beckwith has enjoyed conversations with NFL referees and Sports Illustrated writers and missed by one day some face time with supermodel Kate Upton, who was in town to do a golf photoshoot with Arnold Palmer, who was then 82.

I was sitting near the hotel the day Palmer snuck up behind me and rained noogies on my noggin. It was September 12, 2012, two days after he'd been in Washington to accept the Congressional Medal of Freedom on his 83rd birthday. It'd been eight years after he was there to receive the Presidential Medal of Freedom. Only a few hundred Americans have been deemed worthy of both. So on Monday he was in Washington becoming certifiably one of the greatest Americans to ever live and on Wednesday he was back in Latrobe giving me noogies. I remember struggling to grasp which of the two scenarios was more bewildering. I'm thinking it's still the noogies.

We were among the 200 guests at the hotel party tent to fete him and the new hotel. Palmer was happy the gala would raise tens of thousands of dollars to help life-saving cancer research; I was happy the food and drinks were free. It was toward the end of the affair and at the table where my wife, Val, and I were seated when I felt a strong right arm reach around my neck while the free hand began knuckling my skull. It was Palmer. I asked Val about it later. Did he look angry? Homicidal? "No, he was smiling," she said. "He looked like he was having fun."

So there we were, one of the most consequential men on the planet treating me, one of the least, like we were a couple of junior high school lunch buddies. Billionaire Bill Marriott, also in attendance, must have been envious. It was just the second time Palmer surprised me with a joyful burst of flattering attention. The first involved my favorite Palmer signature—the one he put on the covers of every copy of my 2013 self-help humor book, Use All the Crayons! The Colorful Guide to Simple Human Happiness.

The book is 501 tips on how to make every life more fun, more soulful—more colorful. Tips include No. 399: "Tell friends you're opening an art gallery. Invite them to a big empty room with nothing on the walls. Have them be greeted by 40 guys who say nothing but 'Hi, I'm Art!'" The publisher loved it. My editor said, "You've written an awesome book. It's just so much fun and has a simple, uplifting message that's bound to have wide appeal. Do you happen to know anybody famous who might consider providing a gushy foreword we can use for the cover?"

I told her I'd give it some thought. With Palmer's endorsement, the book earned shelf space in bookstores coast-to-coast and led to fun and lucrative speaking engagements across the country from meeting planners looking to engage their audiences with a soulful message of heart and humor. I used to wonder why Palmer made my silly little book the first of its kind he ever graced with so prominent an endorsement.

I think it comes down to noogies.

He was this incredibly wealthy and successful man so imbued with boyish enthusiasm, so without regal pretense that he thought nothing of bestowing these warm gestures in the midst of a room others would stifle with self-important ceremony. His was a warmth that resonated across all the spectrum of humanity. We're all the better for having the opportunity to bask in its glow.

Garvey was up bright and early the next morning. He was up early enough, in fact, to be the first one at the Latrobe Country Club. He just sat on the porch of the pro shop and was patiently waiting for someone to show up. That someone was affable locker room attendant Frank Silverio. He'd been there 22 years and told Garvey how when he started that Palmer put an arm around him and said, "Frank, you're family now." Head pro Matt Pellis came up with the keys, and Latrobe Country Club was open for business. Garvey asked if he had any tee times. "You're in luck," he said. "We're not busy today."

He asked if he wanted to play by himself or with a member. Being a social gent, he said member. "It started to feel like divine intervention because one of the first men to come along introduced himself as Clark Kerr," Garvey said.

Kerr must have been feeling shy. Most of us know him as Rev. Kerr, minister of the gospel of Jesus Christ at Latrobe Presbyterian Church. Kerr's name was in the national news the week before for presiding at the private funeral for Arnold Daniel Palmer. So it was a fantastic round filled with stories, shared laughter, and promises to keep in touch, the

Arnold Palmer hits a shot out of a bunker on the 12th hole during a practice round at The Masters in 1992, but the golfer's legacy in Latrobe, Pennsylvania, will endure forever. *(Howdy Giles)*

very essence of golf right there at Latrobe Country Club. And it kept getting better.

Since Garvey was dining alone in the Grille Room, some longtime members asked him to join them. He asked each to tell their best Palmer story. It became one of Garvey's best meals ever simply because of the topic and the conversation. He leaned forward when one of the members said, "I don't think I've ever told this story before."

The member told the story he'd heard Palmer tell about the time when then-Governor Ronald Reagan and top GOP strategists flew Palmer to Beverly Hills to ask him if he'd run for president. "He said Reagan told Palmer none of them could stand that SOB Barry Goldwater and didn't want him to be president," Garvey said. "He said Arnie looked around the room and said to Reagan, 'Gee, guys, all I really want to do is play golf.'" He said he was flattered, but the answer was no. Then he asked if they were going to fly him home to Latrobe. They did, and Goldwater got shellacked in the presidential election by President Lyndon Johnson.

The rest of his visit was more golf, more stories, more friends. He was solo, but he never felt alone. Far from it. "I felt like every step I took," Garvey said, "I was side-by-side with my late father and Arnold Palmer."

He was so swept up in the Palmer spirit that the following spring he took another week off and drove to Orlando, Florida, to volunteer to be a marshal at the Arnold Palmer Invitational where he was told he was the only volunteer out of 1,200 who'd come from west of the Mississippi. He said some have marveled, some cynically, that anyone would travel from Oklahoma City to a small town in western Pennsylvania just to play golf. Don't worry, he says, he'll be doing it again—and he hopes to convince the world to follow in his footsteps, in Palmer's footsteps.

"From the day I got there, I just felt like I was where I was supposed to be," he said. "I knew right away I was among friends. Arnold Palmer's Latrobe Country Club is as important to the golf world as St. Andrews. Every golfer should make it a goal to play a round of golf here and walk in the footsteps of an American legend."

Acknowledgments

This book would not have been possible without nearly two decades of steadfast cheer, support, and friendship of Debbie Messich, Gina Varrone, Bob Demangone, Cori Britt, and, especially, Doc Giffin. I consider Doc's friendship one of my life's privileges.

Thanks to everyone who so graciously shared their best Arnold Palmer stories with me. If I was unable to include any of yours, I apologize and hope you'll understand that our conversation and your insights helped shape the result.

Thanks to all the caddies, course owners, head pros, and green superintendents who talked to me. You are the heart and soul of the game that Arnold Palmer loved. And he loved each and every one of you for all you do to help to grow the game.

Because he's a nimble mix of encouragement, foresight, and competence, I was happy to have Jeff Fedotin so deftly edit this book. I'm grateful to Adams Memorial Library in Latrobe for research opportunities and for always being so supportive of my books.

I was delighted when Steve Kittey, editor of the *Latrobe Bulletin*, said not only would the *Bulletin* run the story that I was looking for locals' best Arnold Palmer stories, I was welcome to write it. Steve, that story led to an avalanche of interesting calls, most of which are included in the previous pages. Let other writers have the social media; I'll take the *Bulletin*.

I'm indebted to Buck and Wayne Pawlosky and the staff at The Tin Lizzy for allowing me to call the most interesting and historic building in Westmoreland County my "office."

Thanks to Val, Josie, and Lucy for the daily and everlasting joy your love brings to my life.

Lastly, thanks to Latrobe and its people who for 25 years have made me and my family believe we're right where we ought to be.

Sources

BOOKS

A Golfer's Life, by Arnold Palmer with James Dodson

Hole in One! The Complete Book of Fact, Legend & Lore on Golf's Luckiest Shot, by Chris Rodell

Use All the Crayons! The Colorful Guide to Simple Human Happiness, by Chris Rodell

NEWSPAPERS

Latrobe Bulletin

Tribune-Review of Greensburg

Pittsburgh Post-Gazette

The New York Times

The Washington Post

MAGAZINES

Sports Illustrated

Golf magazine

Golf Digest

Maximum Golf

About the Author

Oddball features could be the two words that sum up my entire career. I started out writing oddball features for newspapers in Nashville and then Greensburg, Pennsylvania, an hour east of my Pittsburgh birthplace and about 10 miles west of my future Latrobe home. I had a flare for finding the fun beneath the surface of standard stories.

There was the story of Darwin, Minnesota, the town saved by a giant ball of twine. Harold Deal was the man who was struck by lightning and never felt cold again, and then there's the story of the blind 72-year-old Everglades gator farmer who still enjoyed rasslin' the killer creatures. There were stories about the biggest, the loudest, the wildest, the strongest, the deepest, the highest—pick your noun—in the whole wide world.

Connoisseurs of sensational storytelling may recognize a root thread of these stories. Yes, I spent from 1992 to 2002 doing more than 1,000 swashbuckling stories for the *National Enquirer*. Understand, I wasn't a Hollywood celebrity reporter. My interest was in people, not personalities. I believe for a writer to succeed he or she needed seasoning with real world experiences. And for all of the publication's notoriety, I was convinced what was a great story for *National Enquirer* would be a great story for *Esquire, Men's Health*, or even *Golf* magazine.

It was all in the telling.

Yet, to hedge my bets, I maintained my contacts in more mainstream publications. I did travel stories for many of the top newspapers, humor essays for regional magazines. And when they changed the name of my home address to Arnold Palmer Drive, I saw an opportunity to write about golf, which meant playing free golf! Golf had always been a big part of my life. It provided my most indelible link to my late father, Paul, a fun, beautiful man whose 2004 death only enhanced my joyful reverence for having been lucky enough to be one of his two sons.

To me, he'll always represent the essential part of golf so sadly neglected in most of today's tech-heavy golf publications.

Paul Rodell played golf because golf is fun. He loved everything about it. He loved to play and he loved to watch others play either on TV or in person. He loved being an amateur meteorologist on the drive to the course: "I think it's gonna clear up!" He loved figuring out the match, the teams, and how many mulligans he was entitled to take.

He cheated but did so obviously and without any intent to fraud, so his sins were always forgiven. I remember asking him if he ever once considered scoring an honest round. "I play golf for my health," he said, "and I feel better when I can tell people I shot a good score."

And for logic like that and a gracious humanity that practically gave off a glow, he was utterly beloved. So, naturally, his writer son began to gravitate toward golf writing—and free golf.

At this point, I must make a confession to satisfy the sticklers: my home was never actually on Arnold Palmer Drive. Stingy township officials stopped the ceremonial designation at the bridge that leads into Youngstown. In fact, my old house—we lived there from 1992 to 2007—was on Main Street. Fred Rogers Way was to the right out our old front door and five houses up. In my defense, no less authority than the United States Postal Service vouched for my deceit. I routinely included the Arnold Palmer Drive address in my correspondence with magazine editors, and they always delivered. And I enjoyed a nice run with top industry publications willing to liven up their pages with non-traditional golf features about things like the future of golf on the moon.

I continued writing non-golf stories for various national publications. I did a story for *Esquire* about a friendly Bellingham, Washington, tavern where three serial killers (Ted Bundy, John Muhammad, and Ken Bianchi) were all at various times regular patrons in good standing. For *Playboy* I did a story about Angelo Cammarata, the world's longest serving bartender. And for *Maxim* I did a cheeky story about beer can astrology, the premise being any beer with a born-on-date was, like human beer drinkers, either an Aquarius, Virgo, Gemini, etc. Bottom line: all beers are compatible with all beer drinkers.

This was all a lot of fun and led to small-time celebrity on Pittsburgh TV and radio stations on the lookout for offbeat giggles. I had by then a treasure chest of great human interest stories. Maybe 10 percent of my workload involved golf features—1 percent of those involving famous golfers who lived within walking distance. I am a very lucky man.

ALSO BY CHRIS RODELL
Fiction
2018
Evan & Elle in Heaven & Hell
A Long-Distance Social Media Afterlife Love Story

2017
The Last Baby Boomer
The Story of the Ultimate Ghoul Pool

Nonfiction
2013
Use All the Crayons!
The Colorful Guide to Simple Human Happiness

2003
Hole in One!
The Complete Book of Fact, Legend & Lore on Golf's Luckiest Shot

Check out Rodell's blog at: www.EightDaysToAmish.com